Anthony Benezet

Some Historical Account of Guinea

Its situation, produce, and the general disposition of its inhabitants, with an inquiry

into the rise and progress of the slave trade, its nature and lamentable effects

Anthony Benezet

Some Historical Account of Guinea

Its situation, produce, and the general disposition of its inhabitants, with an inquiry into the rise and progress of the slave trade, its nature and lamentable effects

ISBN/EAN: 9783337411107

Printed in Europe, USA, Canada, Australia, Japan

Cover: Foto ©ninafisch / pixelio.de

More available books at **www.hansebooks.com**

SOME

HISTORICAL ACCOUNT

OF

GUINEA,

ITS

SITUATION, PRODUCE, and the General
DISPOSITION OF ITS INHABITANTS.

WITH

An Inquiry into the RISE and PROGRESS

OF THE

SLAVE TRADE,

Its NATURE, and Lamentable EFFECTS.

By ANTHONY BENEZET.

Acts xvii. 24. 26. GOD, *that made the world—hath made of* one blood *all nations of men, for to dwell on all the face of the earth, and hath determined the—bounds of their habitation.*

A NEW EDITION.

L O N D O N:

Printed and Sold by J. PHILLIPS, George Yard, Lombard-street.
M. DCC. LXXXVIII.

CONTENTS.

CHAPTER I.

A GENERAL *account of* Guinea; *particularly those parts on the rivers* Senegal *and* Gambia.
Page 1

CHAP. II.

Account of the Ivory-Coast, *the* Gold-Coast, *and the* Slave-Coast. 14

CHAP. III.

Of the kingdoms of Benin, Kongo *and* Angola. 30

CHAP. IV.

Guinea, *first discovered and subdued by the* Arabians. *The* Portuguese *make descents on the coast, and carry off the natives. Oppression of the* Indians: *De la Casa pleads their cause.* 35

CHAP. V.

The first trade of the English *to the coast of* Guinea: *Violently carry off some of the Negroes.* 45

a 3 CHAP.

CHAP. VI.

Slavery more tolerable under Pagans *and* Turks *than in the colonies. As Chriſtianity prevailed, ancient ſlavery declined.* 54

CHAP. VII.

Monteſquieu's *ſentiments of ſlavery.* Morgan Godwyn *advocates the cauſe of the Negroes and Indians, &c.* 62

CHAP. VIII.

Grievous treatment of the Negroes in the colonies, &c. 72

CHAP. IX.

Deſire of gain the true motive of the Slave trade. *Miſrepreſentation of the ſtate of the Negroes in* Guinea. 81

CHAP. X.

State of the Government in Guinea, &c. 88

CHAP. XI.

Accounts of the cruel methods uſed in carrying on the Slave trade, &c. 93

CHAP.

CHAP. XII.

Extracts of several voyages to the coast of Guinea, &c. 99

CHAP. XIII.

Numbers of Negroes yearly brought from Guinea *by the* English, &c. 107

CHAP. XIV.

Observations on the situation and disposition of the Negroes in the Northern colonies, &c. 111

CHAP. XV.

The expediency of a general freedom being granted to the Negroes considered. 116

CHAP. XVI.

Europeans *capable of bearing reasonable labour in the* West Indies, &c. 119

ADVERTISEMENT.

THE Author of the following Account of Guinea having been one of the earlieſt and moſt diſtinguiſhed advocates for the unfortunate Africans, a ſhort account of him may not be unacceptable.

Anthony Benezet was of a reſpectable family, and was born at St. Quintin, in Picardy, in 1713. His father was one of the many Proteſtants who, in conſequence of the perſecutions which followed the revocation of the edict of Nantz, ſought an aſylum in foreign countries. After a ſhort ſtay in Holland, he ſettled with his wife and ſeveral children in London, in 1715.

Our Author having received a liberal education, ſerved an apprenticeſhip in an eminent mercantile houſe in London. In 1731, the whole family removed to Philadelphia. His three brothers followed trade ſuccefsfully; but he, whoſe purſuits were directed to worthier objects than the attainment of wealth, and whoſe higheſt gratification conſiſted in promoting the welfare of mankind, choſe the humble, but uſeful, occupation of inſtructing young people in the paths of knowledge and virtue.

Soon

Soon after his arrival in America, he joined in profession with the people called Quakers. The exertions of that society to annihilate the unchristian practice of holding negroes in slavery, are well known: In these endeavours, it is presumed that no individual took a more active part than this worthy citizen of the world. His writings on this subject were numerous; besides several smaller tracts, which were generally dispersed, he published, in the year 1762, the following Account, of which this is the fourth edition; and in 1767, he also published his "Caution and Warning to Great Britain and her Colonies." With the same benevolent views, he not only availed himself of every opportunity of personal application, but also corresponded with many persons in Europe, America, and the West Indies. Though mean in his personal appearance, such was the courtesy of his manners, and so evident the purity of his intentions, that he had ready access to people of all descriptions, and obtained the respect of the few whom he failed to influence.

About 1756, a considerable number of French families were removed from Acadia to Pennsylvania, on account of some political suspicions. Towards these unfortunate people he manifested his usual philanthropy, and exerted himself much in their behalf; and it was generally to his care that the many contributions, raised to alleviate their distresses, were entrusted. In a country where few understood their language, they were wretched and helpless: circumstances which insured them his cheerful assistance.

Appre-

Apprehending that much advantage would arife, both to the individuals and the publick, from inftructing the black people in common learning, he zealoufly promoted the eftablifhment of a fchool in Philadelphia for that purpofe. His endeavours were fuccefsful, and a fchool for negroes was inftituted, and has been fupported ever fince, principally by the religious fociety of which he was a member; in which however they have been liberally affifted by well-difpofed perfons of other denominations.* The two laft years of his life he devoted to a perfonal attendance of this fchool, being earneftly defirous that the black people might be better qualified for the enjoyment of that freedom to which great numbers of them had then been reftored. To this, which he conceived to be a religious duty, he facrificed the fuperior emoluments of his former fchool, and his bodily eafe, although the weaknefs of his conftitution feemed to demand indulgence. By his laft will he directed, that after the deceafe of his widow, his whole little fortune (the favings of fifty years induftry) fhould, except a few fmall legacies, be applied to the fupport of this Negroe fchool, which had been fo much indebted to his care and benevolence: fome ftriking proofs of the Negroe-children's advancement in learning in this fchool have lately been tranfmitted to England.

---

* Dr. Wilfon, the late Rector of St. Stephens, Walbrook, a fhort time before his deceafe, fent 50l. fterling to him, to be applied to the fupport of this fchool, intending to have doubled the benefaction: but he died before he effected his benevolent purpofe.

The

The year preceding his deceafe, obferving that the flave-trade (which during the war then recently concluded had much declined) was reviving, he addreffed a pathetic letter on the fubject to our amiable Queen, who, on hearing the writer's character, received it with marks of peculiar condefcenfion.

After a few days illnefs, this excellent man died at Philadelphia, in the fpring 1784. The interment of his remains was attended by feveral thoufands of all ranks, profeffions, and parties, who appeared fincerely to unite in deploring the lofs of this friend of mankind. The mournful proceffion was clofed by fome hundreds of thofe poor Negroes, who had been perfonally benefited by his labours, and whofe behaviour on the occafion affectingly evinced their gratitude and affection for their indefatigable benefactor.

INTRO-

INTRODUCTION.

THE slavery of the Negroes having, of late, drawn the attention of many serious minded people, several tracts have been published setting forth its inconsistency with every Christian and moral virtue, which it is hoped will have weight with the judicious; especially at a time when the liberties of mankind are become so much the subject of general attention. For the satisfaction of the serious inquirer, who may not have the opportunity of seeing those tracts, and such others who are sincerely desirous that the iniquity of this practice may become apparent to those in whose power it may be to put a stop to any farther progress therein; and in order to enable the reader to form a

true

true judgment of this matter, which, though so very important, is generally disregarded, or so artfully misrepresented by those whose interest leads them to vindicate it, as to bias the opinions of people otherwise upright, it is proposed to give some account of the different parts of Africa, from which the Negroes are brought to America; with an impartial relation from what motives the Europeans were first induced to undertake, and have since continued this iniquitous traffick. And here it will not be improper to premise, that though wars, arising from the common depravity of human nature, have happened, as well among the Negroes as other nations, and the weak sometimes been made captives to the strong; yet nothing appears in the various relations of the intercourse and trade for a long time carried on by the Europeans on that coast, which would induce us to believe,

lieve, that there is any real foundation for the argument, fo commonly advanced in vindication of the trade, viz. " *That the flavery of the Negroes took its rife from a defire, in the purchafers, to fave the lives of fuch of them as were taken captives in war, who would otherwife have been facrificed to the implacable revenge of their conquerors.*" A plea which, when compared with the hiftory of thofe times, will appear to be deftitute of truth; and to have been advanced, and urged, principally by fuch as were concerned in reaping the gain of this infamous traffick, as a palliation of that, againft which their own reafon and confcience muft have raifed fearful objections.

Some

SOME

HISTORICAL ACCOUNT

OF

GUINEA.

CHAP. I.

GUINEA affords an easy living to its inhabitants, with but little toil. The climate agrees well with the natives, but is extremely unhealthy to the Europeans. Produces provisions in the greatest plenty. Simplicity of their housholdry. The coast of Guinea described from the river Senegal to the kingdom of Angola. The fruitfulness of that part lying on and between the two great rivers Senegal and Gambia. Account of the different nations settled there. Order of Government among the Jalofs. Good account of some of the Fulis. The Mandingos; their management, government, &c. Their worship. M. Adanson's account of those countries. Surprizing vegetation. Pleasant appearance of the country. He found the natives very sociable and obliging.

WHEN the Negroes are considered barely in their present abject state of slavery, broken-spirited and dejected; and too easy credit is given to the accounts we frequently hear or read of their barbarous and savage way of living in their own country; we shall be naturally induced to look upon them as incapable

capable of improvement, deftitute, miferable, and infenfible of the benefits of life; and that our permitting them to live amongft us, even on the moft oppreffive terms, is to them a favour. But, on impartial enquiry, the cafe will appear to be far otherwife; we fhall find that there is fcarce a country in the whole world, that is better calculated for affording the neceffary comforts of life to its inhabitants, with lefs folicitude and toil, than Guinea; and that notwithftanding the long converfe of many of its inhabitants with (often) the worft of the Europeans, they ftill retain a great deal of innocent fimplicity; and, when not ftirred up to revenge from the frequent abufes they have received from the Europeans in general, manifeft themfelves to be a humane, fociable people, whofe faculties are as capable of improvement as thofe of other men; and that their œconomy and government is, in many refpects, commendable. Hence it appears they might have lived happy, if not difturbed by the Europeans; more efpecially, if thefe laft had ufed fuch endeavours as their chriftian profeffion requires, to communicate to the ignorant Africans that fuperior knowledge which providence had favoured them with. In order to fet this matter in its true light, and for the information of thofe well-minded people who are defirous of being fully acquainted with the merits of a caufe, which is of the utmoft confequence; as therein the lives and happinefs of thoufands, and hundreds of thoufands, of our fellow *Men* have fallen, and are daily falling, a facrifice to felfifh avarice and ufurped power, I will here give fome account of the feveral divifions of thofe parts of Africa

from

from whence the Negroes are brought, with a summary of their produce; the disposition of their respective inhabitants, their improvements, &c. &c. extracted from authors of credit; mostly such as have been principal officers in the English, French, and Dutch factories, and who resided many years in those countries. But first it is necessary to premise, as a remark generally applicable to the whole coast of Guinea, "*That the Almighty who has determined, and appointed the bounds of the habitation of men on the face of the earth,*" in the manner that is most conducive to the well-being of their different natures and dispositions, has so ordered it, that although Guinea is extremely unhealthy* to the Europeans, of whom many thousands have met there with a miserable and untimely end,

---

* *Gentleman's Magazine, Supplement,* 1763. *Extract of a letter written from the island of Senegal by Mr Boone, practitioner of physic there, to Dr. Brocklesby of London.*

" To form a just idea of the unhealthiness of the climate, it will be necessary to conceive a country extending three hundred leagues East, and more to the North and South. Through this country several large rivers empty themselves into the sea; particularly the Sanaga, Gambia, and Sherbro; these, during the rainy months, which begin in July, and continue till October, overflow their banks, and lay the whole flat country under water; and indeed the very sudden rise of these rivers is incredible to persons who have never been within the tropicks, and are unacquainted with the violent rains that fall there. At Galem, nine hundred miles from the mouth of the Sanaga, I am informed that the waters rise one hundred and fifty feet perpendicular from the bed of the river. This information I received from a gentleman, " who

end, yet it is not so with the Negroes, who enjoy a good state of health*, and are able to procure to themselves a comfortable subsistence, with much less care and toil than is necessary in our more northern climate; which last advantage arises not only from the warmth of the climate, but also from the overflowing of the rivers, whereby the land is regularly moistened, and

---

" who was surgeon's mate to a party sent there, and the only
" survivor of three captains command, each consisting of
" one captain, two lieutenants, one ensign, a surge-
" on's mate, three sergeants, three corporals, and fifty pri-
" vates.

" When the rains are at an end, which usually hap-
" pens in October, the intense heat of the sun soon dries
" up the waters which lie on the higher parts of the
" earth, and the remainder forms lakes of stagnated waters,
" in which are found all sorts of dead animals: These
" waters every day decrease, till at last they are quite
" exhaled, and then the effluvia that arise are almost in-
" supportable. At this season, the winds blow so very
" hot from off the land, that I can compare them to no-
" thing but the heat proceeding out of the mouth of an
" oven. This occasions the Europeans to be sorely vexed
" with bilious and putrid fevers. From this account you
" will not be surprized, that the total loss of British sub-
" jects in this island only, amounted to above two thou-
" sand five hundred, in the space of three years that I
" was there, in such a putrid moist air as I have describ-
" ed."

* James Barbot, agent general to the French African company, in his account of Africa, page 105, says, " The natives are seldom troubled with any distempers,
" being little affected with the unhealthy air. In tem-
" pestuous times they keep much within doors; and when
" exposed to the weather, their skins being suppled, and
" pores closed by daily anointing with palm oil, the wea-
" ther can make but little impression on them."

and rendered extremely fertile; and being in many places improved by culture, abounds with grain and fruits, cattle, poultry, &c. The earth yields all the year a freſh ſupply of food: Few cloaths are requiſite, and little art neceſſary in making them, or in the conſtruction of their houſes, which are very ſimple, principally calculated to defend them from the tempeſtuous ſeaſons and wild beaſts; a few dry reeds covered with matts ſerve for their beds. The other furniture, except what belongs to cookery, gives the women but little trouble; the moveables of the greateſt among them amounting only to a few earthen pots, ſome wooden utenſils, and gourds or calabaſhes; from theſe laſt, which grow almoſt naturally over their huts, to which they afford an agreeable ſhade, they are abundantly ſtocked with good clean veſſels for moſt houſhold uſes, being of different ſizes, from half a pint to ſeveral gallons.

That part of Africa from which the Negroes are ſold to be carried into ſlavery, commonly known by the name of Guinea, extends along the coaſt three or four thouſand miles. Beginning at the river Senegal, ſituate about the 17th degree of North latitude, being the neareſt part of Guinea, as well to Europe as to North America; from thence to the river Gambia, and in a ſoutherly courſe to Cape Sierra Leona, comprehends a coaſt of about ſeven hundred miles; being the ſame tract for which Queen Elizabeth granted charters to the firſt traders to that coaſt. From Sierra Leona, the land of Guinea takes a turn to the eaſtward, extending that courſe about fifteen hundred miles, including

ing those several divisions known by the name of *the Grain Coast, the Ivory Coast, the Gold Coast, and the Slave Coast, with the large kingdom of Benin.* From thence the land runs southward along the coast about twelve hundred miles, which contains the *kingdoms of Congo and Angola;* there the trade for slaves ends. From which to the southermost Cape of Africa, called the Cape of Good Hope, the country is settled by Caffres and Hottentots, who have never been concerned in the making or selling slaves.

Of the parts which are above described, the first which presents itself to view, is that situate on the great river Senegal, which is said to be navigable more than a thousand miles, and is by travellers described to be very agreeable and fruitful. Andrew Brue, principal factor to the French African company, who lived sixteen years in that country, after describing its fruitfulness and plenty, near the sea, adds*, " The farther you go from the sea, the country " on the river seems the more fruitful and well " improved; abounding with Indian corn, " pulse, fruit, &c. Here are vast meadows, " which feed large herds of great and small " cattle, and poultry numerous. The villages " that lie thick on the river, shew the country " is well peopled." The same author, in the account of a voyage he made up the river Gambia, the mouth of which lies about three hundred miles South of the Senegal, and is navigable about six hundred miles up the country,

says,

---

* Astley's Collect. vol. 2. page 46.

says*, "That he was surprized to see the land so well cultivated; scarce a spot lay unimproved; the low lands, divided by small canals, were all sowed with rice, &c. the higher ground planted with millet, Indian corn, and pease of different sorts; their beef excellent; poultry plenty, and very cheap, as well as all other necessaries of life." Francis Moor, who was sent from England about the year 1735, in the service of the African company, and resided at James Fort, on the river Gambia, or in other factories on that river, about five years, confirms the above account of the fruitfulness of the country. William Smith, who was sent in the year 1726, by the African Company, to survey their settlements throughout the whole coast of Guinea, § says, "The country about the Gambia is pleasant and fruitful; provisions of all kinds being plenty, and exceeding cheap." The country on and between the two above-mentioned rivers is large and extensive, inhabited principally by those three Negroe nations known by the name of Jalofs, Fulis, and Mandingos. The Jalofs possess the middle of the country. The Fulis principal settlement is on both sides of the Senegal; great numbers of these people are also mixed with the Mandingos; which last are mostly settled on both sides the Gambia. The government of the Jalofs is represented as under a better regulation than can be expected from the common opinion we entertain

---

* Astley's Collection of Voyages, vol. 2, page 86,
§ William Smith's Voyage to Guinea, page 31, 34.

entertain of the Negroes. We are told in the Collection, * " That the King has under him se-
" veral ministers of state, who assist him in the ex-
" ercise of justice. *The grand Jerafo* is the chief
" justice through all the King's dominions, and
" goes in circuit from time to time to hear com-
" plaints, and determine controversies. *The*
" *King's treasurer* exercises the same employment,
" and has under him Alkairs, who are governors
" of towns or villages. That the *Kondi,* or
" *Viceroy,* goes the circuit with the chief justice,
" both to hear causes, and inspect into the be-
" haviour of the *Alkadi,* or chief magistrate of
" every village in their several districts §."
Vasconcelas, an author mentioned in the Collection, says, " the ancientest are preferred to
" be the *Prince's counsellors,* who keep always
" about his person; and the men of most judg-
" ment and experience are the judges." The
Fulis are settled on both sides of the river
Senegal: their country, which is very fruitful
and populous, extends near four hundred miles
from East to West. They are generally of a
deep tawney complexion, appearing to bear some
affinity with the Moors, whose country they join
on the North. They are good farmers, and
make good harvest of corn, cotton, tobacco, &c.
and breed great numbers of cattle of all kinds.
Bartholomew Stibbs, (mentioned by *Fr. Moor*)
in his account of that country says, * " *They*
" *were a cleanly, decent, industrious people, and very*
" *affable.*"

---

* Astley's Collection, vol 2. page 358.
§ Idem. 259.
♥ Moor's Travels into distant parts of Africa, page 198.

" *affable.*" But the moſt particular account we have of theſe people, is from *Francis Moor* himſelf, who ſays*, " Some of theſe Fuli blacks, " who dwell on both ſides the river Gambia, " are in ſubjection to the Mandingos, amongſt " whom they dwell, having been probably driven " out of their country by war or famine. They " have chiefs of their own, who rule with " much moderation. Few of them will drink " brandy, or any thing ſtronger than water " and ſugar, being ſtrict Mahometans. Their " form of government goes on eaſy, becauſe " the people are of a good quiet diſpoſition, " and ſo well inſtructed in what is right, that a " man who does ill, is the abomination of all, " and none will ſupport him againſt the chief. " In theſe countries, the natives are not co- " vetous of land, deſiring no more than what " they uſe; and as they do not plough with " horſes and cattle, they can uſe but very little, " therefore the Kings are willing to give the " Fulis leave to live in the country, and cul- " tivate their lands. If any of their people " are known to be made ſlaves, all the Fulis " will join to redeem them; they alſo ſupport " the old, the blind, and lame, amongſt them- " ſelves; and as far as their abilities go, they " ſupply the neceſſities of the Mandingos, great " numbers of whom they have maintained in " famine." *The author*, from his own obſervations, ſays, " They were rarely angry, and " that he never heard them abuſe one another."

---

* Ibid, page 21.

The Mandingos are said by *A. Brue* before mentioned, "To be the moft numerous nation "on the Gambia, befides which, numbers of "them are difperfed over all thefe countries; "being the moft rigid Mahometans among the "Negroes, they drink neither wine nor brandy, "and are politer than the other Negroes. The "chief of the trade goes through their hands. "Many are induftrious and laborious, keep- "ing their ground well cultivated, and breed- "ing a good ftock of cattle*. Every town "has an *Alkadi*, or *Governor*, who has great "power; for moft of them having two com- "mon fields of clear ground, one for corn, "and the other for rice, *the Alkadi* appoints "the labour of all the people. The men "work the corn ground, and the women and "girls the rice ground; and as they all "equally labour, fo he equally divides the "corn amongft them; and in cafe they are "in want, the others fupply them. This Al- "kadi decides all quarrels, and has the firft "voice in all conferences in town affairs." Some of thefe Mandingos who are fettled at Galem, far up the river Senegal, can read and write Arabic tolerably, and are a good hofpitable people, who carry on a trade with the inland nations. "† They are extremely populous in "thofe parts, their women being fruitful, and "they not fuffering any perfon amongft them, "but fuch as are guilty of crimes, to be made "flaves."

---

* Aftley's Collect. vol. 2. page 269.
† Aftley's Collect. vol. 2. page 73.

"slaves." We are told from Jobson, "‡ That
"the Mahometan Negroes say their prayers thrice
"a day. Each village has a priest who calls them
"to their duty. It is surprizing (says the author)
"as well as commendable, to see the modesty, at-
"tention and reverence they observe during
"their worship. He asked some of their priests
"the purport of their prayers and ceremonies;
"their answer always was, *That they adored God
"by prostrating themselves before him; that by
"humbling themselves, they acknowledged their
"own insignificancy, and farther intreated him to
"forgive their faults, and to grant them all good
"and necessary things as well as deliverance from
"evil.*" Jobson takes notice of several good
qualities in these Negroe priests, particularly
their great sobriety. They gain their livelihood
by keeping school for the education of the children. The boys are taught to read and write.
They not only teach school, but rove about the
country, teaching and instructing, for which
the whole country is open to them; and they
have a free course through all places, though
the Kings may be at war with one another.

The three fore-mentioned nations practise several trades, as smiths, potters, sadlers, and
weavers. Their smiths particularly work neatly
in gold and silver, and make knives, hatchets,
reaping hooks, spades and shares to cut iron,
&c. &c. Their potters make neat tobacco
pipes, and pots to boil their food. Some authors say that weaving is their principal trade;
this

‡ Ibid. 296.

this is done by the women and girls, who spin and weave very fine cotton cloth, which they dye blue or black. * F. Moor says, the Jalofs particularly make great quantities of the cotton cloth; their pieces are generally twenty-seven yards long, and about nine inches broad, their looms being very narrow.; these they sew neatly together, so as to supply the use of broad cloth.

It was in these parts of Guinea, that M. Adanson, correspondent of the Royal Academy of Sciences at Paris, mentioned in some former publications, was employed from the year 1749, to the year 1753, wholly in making *natural* and *philosophical* observations on the country about the rivers Senegal and Gambia. Speaking of the great heats in Senegal, he says, " † It is " to them that they are partly indebted for the " fertility of their lands; which is so great, " that, with little labour and care, there is " no fruit nor grain but grow in great plenty."

Of the soil on the Gambia, he says, " ‡ It is " rich and deep, and amazingly fertile; it pro- " duces spontaneously, and almost without cul- " tivation, all the necessaries of life, grain, fruit, " herbs, and roots. Every thing matures to " perfection, and is excellent in its kind.*" One thing which always surprized him, was the prodigious rapidity with which the sap of trees repairs

---

* F. Moor, 28.
† M. Adanson's Voyage to Senegal, &c. page 308.
‡ Idem, page :64.
* M. Adanson, page 162.

repairs any lofs they may happen to fuftain in that country : " And I was never," fays he, " more " aftonifhed, than when landing four days after " the locufts had devoured all the fruits and " leaves, and even the buds of the trees, to " find the trees covered with new leaves, and " they did not feem to me to have fuffered " much." §" It was then," fays the fame author, " the fifh feafon; you might fee them in " fhoals approaching towards land. Some of " thofe fhoals were fifty fathom fquare, and " the fifh crouded together in fuch a manner, " as to roll upon one another, without being able " to fwim. As foon as the Negroes perceive " them coming towards land, they jump into the " water with a bafket in one hand, and fwim " with the other. They need only to plunge " and to lift up their bafket, and they are fure " to return loaded with fifh." Speaking of the appearance of the country, and of the difpofition of the people, he fays, ‖ " Which way " foever I turned mine eyes on this pleafant " fpot, I beheld a perfect image of pure nature; " an agreeable folitude, bounded on every fide " by charming landfcapes; the rural fituation " of cottages in the midft of trees; the eafe and " indolence of the Negroes, reclined under the " fhade of their fpreading foliage; the fimpli- " city of their drefs and manners; the whole " revived in my mind the idea of our firft " parents, and I feemed to contemplate the " world in its primitive ftate. They are, ge-
" nerally

---

§ Idem, page 171.　　‖ Ibid, page 54.

"nerally speaking, very good-natured, sociable,
"and obliging. I was not a little pleased with
"this my first reception; it convinced me,
"that there ought to be a considerable abate-
"ment made in the accounts I had read and
"heard every where of the savage character of
"the Africans. I observed both in Negroes and
"Moors, great humanity and sociableness, which
"gave me strong hopes that I should be very
"safe amongst them, and meet with the success
"I desired in my enquiries after the curiosities
"of the country*." He was agreeably a-
mused with the conversation of the Negroes, their
fables, *dialogues*, and *witty stories* with which they
entertain each other alternately, according to
their custom. Speaking of the remarks which
the natives made to him, with relation to the
stars and *planets*, he says, " It is amazing, that
"such a rude and illiterate people, should reason
"so pertinently in regard to those heavenly
"bodies; there is no manner of doubt, but that
"with proper instruments, and a good will,
"they would become *excellent astronomers*."

C H A P. II.

THE Ivory Coast; its soil and produce. The character of the *natives* misrepresented by some authors. These misrepresentations occasioned by *the Europeans* having treacherously carried off

---

* Adanson, page 252, ibid.

off many of their people. *John Smith, Surveyor to the African company,* his obfervations thereon. *John Snock's* remarks. The *Gold Coaſt* and *Slave Coaſt* have the moſt *European factories,* and furniſh the greateſt number of ſlaves to *the Europeans.* Exceeding fertile. The country of *Axim,* and of *Ante.* Good account of the *inland people.* Great fiſhery. Extraordinary trade for ſlaves. The *Slave Coaſt.* The *kingdom of Widah.* Fruitful and pleaſant. The natives kind and obliging. Very populous. Keep regular markets and fairs. Good order therein. Murder, adultery, and theft ſeverely puniſhed. The King's revenues. The principal people have an idea of the true God. Commendable care of the poor. Several ſmall governments depend on *plunder* and the *ſlave* trade.

THAT part of Guinea known by the name of the *Grain,* and *Ivory Coaſt,* comes next in courſe. This coaſt extends about five hundred miles. The ſoil appears by account, to be in general fertile, producing abundance of rice and roots; indigo and cotton thrive without cultivation, and tobacco would be excellent, if carefully manufactured; they have fiſh in plenty; their flocks greatly increaſe, and their trees are loaded with fruit. They make a cotton cloth, which ſells well on the coaſt. In a word, the country is rich, and the commerce advantageous, and might be greatly augmented by ſuch as would cultivate the friendſhip of the natives. Theſe are repreſented by ſome writers as a rude, *treacherous people,* whilſt ſeveral other *authors* of
credit

credit give them a very different character, representing them as *sensible, courteous, and the fairest traders on the coast of Guinea*. In the Collection, they are said * to be averse to drinking to excess, and such as do, are severely punished by the King's order: On enquiry why there is such a disagreement in the character given of these people, it appears, that though they are naturally inclined to be *kind to strangers*, with whom they are *fond* of *trading*, yet the *frequent injuries* done them by Europeans, have occasioned their being *suspicious and shy*: The same cause has been the occasion of the ill treatment they have sometimes given to innocent strangers, who have attempted to trade with them. As the Europeans have no settlement on this part of Guinea, the trade is carried on by signals from the ships, on the appearance of which the natives usually come on board in their canoes, bringing their gold-dust, ivory, &c. which has given opportunity to some villainous Europeans to carry them off with their effects, or retain them on board till a ransom is paid. It is noted by some, that since the European voyagers have carried away several of these people, their mistrust is so great, that it is very difficult to prevail on them to come on board. *William Smith* remarks, "† As we passed
" along this coast, we very often lay before
" a town, and fired a gun for the natives
" to come off, but no soul came near us;
" at length we learnt by some ships that were
trading

---

* Collection, vol 2. page 560.
† W. Smith, page 111.

"trading down the coast, that the natives
"came seldom on board an English ship, for
"fear of being detained or carried off; yet
"at last some ventured on board; but if these
"chanced to spy any arms, they would all im-
"mediately take to their canoes, and make the
"best of their way home. They had then in
"their possession one *Benjamin Cross*, the mate
"of an English vessel, who was detained by
"them to make reprisals for some of their
"men, who had formerly been carried away
"by some English vessel." In the Collection we
are told, § *This villainous custom is too often
practised, chiefly by the Bristol and Liverpool ships,
and is a great detriment to the slave trade on the
windward coast. John Snock, mentioned in Bosman* ‖,
when on that coast, wrote, " We cast anchor,
" but not one Negroe coming on board, I went
" on shore, and after having staid a while on the
" strand, some Negroes came to me; and being
" desirous to be informed why they did not
" come on board, I was answered, that about
" two months before, the English had been
" there with two large vessels, and had ravaged
" the country, destroyed all their canoes, plun-
" dered their houses, and carried off some of
" their people, upon which the remainder fled
" to the inland country, where most of them
" were at that time; so that there not being
" much to be done by us, we were obliged to
" return on board. * When I enquired after
" their

---

§ Astley's Collection, vol. 2. page 475.
‖ W. Bosman's Description of Guinea, page 440.
* W. Bosman's Description of Guinea, page 439.

" their wars with other countries, they told me
" they were not often troubled with them; but
" if any difference happened, they chose rather
" to end the dispute amicably, than come to
" arms. §" He found the inhabitants civil and
good natured. Speaking of the *King of Rio Sestro*,
lower down the coast, he says, " He was a very
" agreeable, obliging man, and all his subjects
" civil, as well as very laborious in agricul-
" ture, and the pursuits of trade." *Marchais*
says, † " That though the country is very popu-
" lous, yet none of the natives except criminals
" are sold for slaves." *Vaillant* never heard of
any settlement being made by the Europeans
on this part of *Guinea*; and *Smith* remarks,
* " That these coasts, which are divided into
" several little kingdoms, have seldom any wars,
" which is the reason the slave trade is not so
" good here as on *the Gold and Slave Coast*,
" where the Europeans have several forts and
" factories." A plain evidence this, that it is
the intercourse with the Europeans, and their
settlements on the coast, which give life to the
slave trade.

Next adjoining to the *Ivory Coast*, are those
called the *Gold Coast*, and the *Slave Coast*; authors are not agreed about their bounds, but
their extent together along the coast may be
about five hundred miles. And as the policy,
produce, and œconomy of these two kingdoms

of

---

§ Ibid. 441.   † Astley's Collection, vol. 2. page 565:
* Smith's voyage to Guinea, page 112.

of Guinea are much the same, I shall describe them together.

Here the Europeans have the greatest number of forts and factories, from whence, by means of the Negro factors, a trade is carried on about seven hundred miles back in the inland country; whereby great numbers of slaves are procured as well by means of the wars which arise amongst the Negroes, or are fomented by the Europeans, as those brought from the back country. Here we find the natives *more reconciled to the European manners and trade*; but, at the same time, *much more inured to war*, and ready to assist the European traders in procuring loadings for the great number of vessels which come yearly on those coasts for slaves. This part of Guinea is agreed by historians to be, in general, *extraordinary fruitful and agreeable*; producing (according to the difference of the soil) vast quantities of rice and other grain; plenty of fruit and roots; palm wine and oil, and fish in great abundance, with much tame and wild cattle. Bosman, principal factor for the Dutch at D'Elmina, speaking of the country of Axim, which is situate near the beginning of the Gold Coast, says*, " The Negro inhabitants are
" generally very rich, driving a great trade with
" the Europeans for gold: That they are in-
" dustriously employed either in trade, fishing,
" or agriculture; but chiefly in the culture of
" rice, which grows here in an incredible
" abundance, and is transported hence all over

" the

---

* Bosman's Description of the Coast of Guinea, p. 5.

" the Gold Coaft. The inhabitants, in lieu,
" returning full fraught with millet, yams,
" potatoes, and palm oil." The fame author
fpeaking of the country of Ante, fays †,
" This country,, as well as the Gold Coaft,
" abounds with hills, enriched with extra-
" ordinary high and beautiful trees; its valleys,
" betwixt the hills, are wide and extenfive, pro-
" ducing in great abundance very good rice,
" millet, yams, potatoes, and other fruits, all
" good in their kind." He adds, " In fhort, it
" is a land that yields its manurers as plentiful
" a crop as they can wifh, with great quantities
" of palm wine and oil, befides being well fur-
" nifhed with all forts of tame, as well as wild
" beafts; but that the laft fatal wars had re-
" duced it to a miferable condition, and ftrip-
" ped it of moft of its inhabitants." The adjoining country of Fetu, he fays *, " was
" formerly fo powerful and populous, that it
" ftruck terror into all the neighbouring na-
" tions; but it is at prefent fo drained by con-
" tinual wars, that it is entirely ruined; there
" does not remain inhabitants fufficient to till
" the country, though it is fo fruitful and plea-
" fant that it may be compared to the country
" of Ante juft before defcribed. Frequently,
" fays that author, when walking through it
" before the laft war, I have feen it abound
" with fine well built and populous towns,
" agreeably enriched with vaft quantities of
" corn,

---

† Bofman's Defcription of the Coaft of Guinea, p. 14.
* Bofman, page 41.

" corn, cattle, palm-wine, and oil. The inha-
" bitants all applying themselves without any
" distinction to agriculture; some sow corn,
" others press oil, and draw wine from palm
" trees, with both which it is plentifully stored."

William Smith gives much the same account of the before-mentioned parts of the Gold Coast, and adds, " The country about D'Elmina and
" Cape Coast, is much the same for beauty and
" goodness, but more populous; and the nearer
" we come towards the Slave Coast, the more
" delightful and rich all the countries are, pro-
" ducing all sorts of trees, fruits, roots, and
" herbs, that grow within the Torrid Zone."

J. Barbot also remarks*, with respect to the countries of Ante and Adom, " That the soil is
" very good, and fruitful in corn and other
" produce, which it affords in such plenty, that
" besides what serves for their own use, they
" always export great quantities for sale; they
" have a competent number of cattle, both
" tame and wild, and the rivers are abundantly
" stored with fish, so that nothing is wanting
" for the support of life, and to make it easy."

In the Collection it is said †, " That the inland
" people on that part of the coast, employ
" themselves in tillage and trade, and supply
" the market with corn, fruit, and palm wine;
" the country producing such vast plenty of
" Indian corn, that abundance is daily exported,
" as well by Europeans as Blacks resorting thi-
" ther

---

* John Barbot's Description of Guinea, page 154.
† Astley's Collect. vol. 2. page 535.

"ther from other parts." "These inland peo-
"ple are said to live in great union and friend-
"ship, being generally well tempered, civil,
"and tractable; not apt to shed human blood,
"(except when much provoked,) and ready to
"assist one another." In the Collection * it is
said, " That the fishing business is esteemed
"on the Gold Coast next to trading; that those
"who profess it are more numerous than those
"of other employments. That the greatest
"number of these are at Kommendo, Mina,
"and Kormantin; from each of which places,
"there go out every morning, (Tuesday ex-
"cepted, which is the Fetish day, or day of rest)
"five, six, and sometimes eight hundred canoes,
"from thirteen to fourteen feet long, which
"spread themselves two leagues at sea, each
"fisherman carrying in his canoe a sword, with
"bread, water, and a little fire on a large stone
"to roast fish. Thus they labour till noon,
"when the sea breeze blowing fresh, they re-
"turn to the shore, generally laden with fish;
"a quantity of which the inland inhabitants
"come down to buy, which they sell again at
"the country markets."

William Smith says ‡, " The country about
"Acra, where the English and Dutch have
"each a strong fort, is very delightful, and
"the natives courteous and civil to strangers."
He adds, " That this place seldom fails of an
"extraordinary good trade from the inland
 "country,

---

* Collection, vol. 2. page 640.
‡ William Smith, page 135.

"country, especially for slaves, whereof several
"are supposed to come from very remote parts,
"because it is not uncommon to find a Malayan
"or two amongst a parcel of other slaves: The
"Malaya people are generally natives of Ma-
"lacca, in the East Indies, situate several thou-
"sand miles from the Gold Coast." They dif-
fer very much from the Guinea Negroes, being
of a tawny complexion, with long black hair.

Most parts of the Slave Coasts are represented as equally fertile and pleasant with the Gold Coast: The kingdom of Whidah has been particularly noted by travellers. * William Smith and Bosman agree, "That it is one of the most
"delightful countries in the world. The great
"number and variety of tall, beautiful, and
"shady trees, which seem planted in groves;
"the verdant fields every where cultivated, and
"no otherwise divided than by those groves,
"and in some places a small foot-path, to-
"gether with a great number of villages, con-
"tribute to afford the most delightful prospect;
"the whole country being a fine, easy, and
"almost imperceptible ascent, for the space of
"forty or fifty miles from the sea. That the
"farther you go from the sea, the more beau-
"tiful and populous the country appears. That
"the natives were kind and obliging, and so
"industrious, that no place which was thought
"fertile, could escape being planted, even
"within the hedges which inclose their villages.
"And

---

* Smith, page 194. Bosman, page 310.

"And that the next day after they had reaped,
"they sowed again."

Snelgrave also says, "The country appears
"full of towns and villages; and being a rich
"soil, and well cultivated, looks like an entire
"garden." In the Collection*, the husbandry of
the Negroes is described to be carried on with
great regularity: "The rainy season approach-
"ing, they go into the fields and woods, to fix
"on a proper place for sowing; and as here is
"no property in ground, the King's licence be-
"ing obtained, the people go out in troops, and
"first clear the ground from bushes and weeds,
"which they burn. The field thus cleared,
"they dig it up a foot deep, and so let it
"remain for eight or ten days, till the rest of
"their neighbours have disposed their ground
"in the same manner. They then consult about
"sowing, and for that end assemble at the
"King's Court the next Fetish day. The King's
"grain must be sown first. They then go again
"to the field, and give the ground a second
"digging, and sow their seed. Whilst the King
"or Governor's land is sowing, he sends out
"wine and flesh ready dressed, enough to serve
"the labourers. Afterwards, they in like man-
"ner sow the ground allotted for their neigh-
"bours, as diligently as that of the King's, by
"whom they are also feasted; and so continue
"to work in a body for the public benefit, till
"every man's ground is tilled and sowed. None
"but the King, and a few great men, are ex-
"empted

---

* Collection, vol. 2. page 651.

" empted from this labour. Their grain soon
" sprouts out of the ground. When it is about
" a man's height, and begins to ear, they raise a
" wooden house in the centre of the field,
" covered with straw, in which they set their
" children to watch their corn, and fright away
" the birds."

Bosman * speaks in commendation of the civility, kindness, and great industry of the natives of Whidah; this is confirmed by Smith †, who says, " The natives here seem to be the most
" gentlemen-like Negroes in Guinea, abound-
" ing with good manners and ceremony to each
" other. The inferior pay the utmost deference
" and respect to the superior, as do wives to
" their husbands, and children to their parents.
" All here are naturally industrious, and find
" constant employment; the men in agriculture,
" and the women in spinning and weaving cot-
" ton. The men, whose chief talent lies in
" husbandry, are unacquainted with arms;
" otherwise, being a numerous people, they
" could have made a better defence against the
" King of Dahome, who subdued them without
" much trouble." " * Throughout the Gold
" Coast, there are regular markets in all villages,
" furnished with provisions and merchandize,
" held every day in the week, except Tuesday,
" whence they supply not only the inhabitants,
" but the European ships. The *Negroe women*
" are very expert in buying and selling, and ex-
" tremely industrious; for they will repair daily
" to

---

* Bosman, page 317.   † Smith, page 157.
● Collect. vol. 2. p. 657.

" to market from a confiderable diftance, load-
" ed like pack horfes, with a child, perhaps, at
" their back, and a heavy burthen on their heads.
" After felling their wares, they buy fifh and
" other neceffaries, and return home loaded as
" they came.

" † There is a market held at Sabi every
" fourth day, alfo a weekly one in the province
" of Aplogua, which is fo reforted to, that there
" are ufually five or fix thoufand merchants.
" Their markets are fo well regulated and
" governed, that feldom any diforder happens;
" each fpecies of merchandize and merchants
" have a feparate place allotted them by them-
" felves. The buyers may haggle as much as
" they will, but it muft be without noife or
" fraud. To keep order, the King appoints a
" judge, who, with four officers well armed,
" infpects the markets, hears all complaints,
" and, in a fummary way, decides all differ-
" ences; he has power to feize, and fell as
" flaves, all who are catched in ftealing, or dif-
" turbing the peace. In thefe markets are to be
" fold men, women, children, oxen, fheep,
" goats, and fowls of all kinds; European cloths,
" linen and woollen; printed callicoes, filk,
" grocery ware, china, gold-duft, iron in bars,
" &c. in a word, moft forts of European goods,
" as well as the produce of Africa and Afia.
" They have other markets, refembling our
" fairs, once or twice a year, to which all the
" country repair; for they take care to order the
                                             " day

---

† Collect. vol. 3. p. 11.

"day so in different governments, as not to in-
"terfere with each other."

With respect to government, William Smith says *, "That the Gold Coast and Slave Coast "are divided into different districts, some of "which are governed by their Chiefs, or Kings; "the others, being more of the nature of a "commonwealth, are governed by some of the "principal men, called Caboceros, who, Bosman "says, are properly denominated civil fathers, "whose province is to take care of the welfare "of the city or village, and to appease tu-"mults." But this order of government has been much broken since the coming of the Europeans. Both Bosman and Barbot mention *murder and adultery to be severely punished on the Coast, frequently by death; and robbery by a fine proportionable to the goods stolen.*

The income of some of the Kings is large. Bosman says, "That the King of Whidah's re-"venues and duties on things bought and sold "are considerable; he having the tithe of all "things sold in the market, or imported in the "country." * Both the above-mentioned authors say, *The tax on slaves shipped off in this King's dominions, in some years, amounts to near twenty thousand pounds.*

Bosman tells us, "The Whidah Negroes have "a faint idea of a true God, ascribing to him "the attributes of almighty power and omni-"presence; but God, they say, is too high to "condescend to think of mankind; wherefore
"he

---

* Smith, page 193.
* Bosman, page 337. Barbot, page 335.

"he commits the government of the world to
"those inferior deities which they worship."
Some authors say, the wisest of these Negroes
are sensible of their mistake in this opinion, but
dare not forsake their own religion, for fear of
the populace rising and killing them. This is
confirmed by William Smith, who says, "That
"all the natives of this coast believe there is
"one true God, the author of them and all
"things; that they have some apprehensions of
"a future state; and that almost every village
"has a grove, or public place of worship, to
"which the principal inhabitants, on a set day,
"resort to make their offerings."

In the Collection * it is remarked as an excellency in the Guinea government, "That
"however poor they may be in general, yet
"there are no beggars to be found amongst
"them; which is owing to the care of their
"chief men, whose province it is to take care
"of the welfare of the city or village; it be-
"ing part of their office, to see that such peo-
"ple may earn their bread by their labour;
"some are set to blow the smith's bellows,
"others to press palm oil, or grind colours for
"their mats, and sell provisions in the markets.
"The young men are lifted to serve as soldiers,
"so that they suffer no common beggar."
Bosman ascribes a further reason for this good
order, viz. "That when a Negroe finds he
"cannot subsist, he binds himself for a certain
"sum of money, and the master to whom he is
"bound

---

* Astley's Collection, vol. 2. page 619.

" bound is obliged to find him neceffaries; that
" the mafter fets him a fort of tafk, which is
" not in the leaft flavifh, being chiefly to defend
" his mafter on occafions; or in fowing time to
" work as much as he himfelf pleafes *."

Adjoining to the kingdom of Whidah, are feveral fmall governments, as Coto, Great and Small Popo, Ardrah, &c. all fituate on the Slave Coaft, where the chief trade for flaves is carried on. Thefe are governed by their refpective Kings, and follow much the fame cuftoms with thofe of Whidah, except that their principal living is on plunder, and the flave trade.

* Bofman, page 119.

CHAP.

C H A P. III.

THE kingdom of Benin; its extent. Esteemed the most potent in Guinea. Fruitfulness of the soil. Good disposition of the people. Order of government. Punishment of crimes. Large extent of the town of Great Benin. Order maintained. The Natives honest and charitable. Their religion. The kingdoms of Kongo and Angola. Many of the natives profess Christianity. The country fruitful. Disposition of the people. The administration of justice. The town of Loango. Slave trade carried on by the Portugueze. Here the slave trade ends.

NEXT adjoining to the Slave Coast, is the kingdom of Benin, which, though it extends but about 170 miles on the sea, yet spreads so far inland, as to be esteemed the most potent kingdom in Guinea. By accounts, the soil and produce appear to be in a great measure like those before described, and the natives are represented as a reasonable good-natured people. Artus says §, " They are a sincere, inoffensive " people, and do no injustice either to one " another, or to strangers." William Smith* confirms this account, and says, " That the in- " habitants are generally very good-natured, " and exceeding courteous and civil. When the
" Europeans

---

§ Collection, vol. 3. page 228.
* Smith, page 228.

"Europeans make them prefents, which in their coming thither to trade they always do, they endeavour to return them doubly."

Bofman tells us†, "That his countrymen the Dutch, who were often obliged to truft them till they returned the next year, were fure to be paid honeftly their whole debts."

There is in Benin a confiderable order in government. Theft, murder, and adultery, being feverely punifhed. Barbot fays ‡, "If a man and a woman of any quality be furprized in adultery, they are both put to death: and their bodies are thrown on a dunghill, and left there a prey to wild beafts." He adds, "The feverity of the laws in Benin againft adultery†,

"amongft

---

† W. Bofman, page 405.
‡ Barbot, page 237.
† By this account of the punifhment inflicted on adulterers in this and other parts of Guinea, it appears the Negroes are not infenfible of the finfulnefs of fuch practices. How ftrange muft it then appear to the ferious minded amongft thefe people, (nay, how inconfiftent is it with every divine and moral law amongft ourfelves) that thofe Chriftian laws, which prohibit fornication and adultery, are in none of the Englifh governments extended to them, but that they are allowed to cohabit and feparate at pleafure? And that even their mafters think fo lightly of their marriage engagements, that, when it fuits with their intereft, they will feparate man from wife, and children from both, to be fold into different and even diftant parts, without regard to their (fometimes) grievous lamentations; whence it has happened, that fuch of thofe people who are truly united in their marriage covenant, and in affection to one another, have been driven to fuch defperation, as either violently to deftroy themfelves, or gradually to pine away, and die with mere grief. It is amazing, that whilft the clergy of the eftablifhed church are publicly

" amongst all orders of people, deters them from
" venturing, so that it is but very seldom any
" persons are punished for that crime." Smith
says, " Their towns are governed by officers
" appointed by the King, who have power to
" decide in civil cases, and to raise the public
" taxes; but in criminal cases, they must send
" to the King's court, which is held at the town
" of Oedo, or Great Benin. This town, which
" covers a large extent of ground, is about sixty
" miles from the sea."   * Barbot tells us,
" That it contains thirty streets, twenty fathom
" wide, and almost two miles long, commonly
" extending in a straight line from one gate to
" another; that the gates are guarded by soldi-
" ers; that in these streets markets are held every
" day, for cattle, ivory, cotton, and many sorts
" of European goods. This large town is di-
" vided into several wards, or districts, each
" governed by its respective king of a street, as
" they call them, to administer justice, and to
" keep good order. The inhabitants are very
" civil and good natured, condescending to what
" the Europeans require of them in a civil way."
The same author confirms what has been said by
others of their justice in the payment of their
debts; and adds, " That they, above all other
" Guineans, are very honest and just in their
                                        " dealings;

---

licly expressing a concern, that these oppressed people should
be made acquainted with the Christian religion, they should
be thus suffered, and even forced, so flagrantly to infringe
one of the principal injunctions of our holy religion!
    * J. Barbot, page 358, 359.

"dealings; and they have such an aversion for theft, that by the law of the country it is punished with death." We are told by the same author‖, " That the King of Benin is able upon occasion to maintain an army of one hundred thousand men; but that for the most part he does not keep thirty thousand." William Smith says, " The natives are all free men; none but foreigners can be bought and sold there†. They are very charitable, the King as well as his subjects." Bosman confirms this‡, and says, " The king and great lords subsist several poor at their place of residence on charity, employing those who are fit for any work, and the rest they keep for God's sake; so that here are no beggars."

As to religion, these people believe there is a God, the efficient cause of all things; but like the rest of the Guineans, they are superstitiously and idolatrously inclined.

The last division of Guinea from which slaves are imported, are the kingdoms of Kongo and Angola; these lie to the south of Benin, extending with the intermediate land about twelve hundred miles on the coast. Great numbers of the natives of both these kingdoms profess the Christian religion, which was long since introduced by the Portugueze, who made early settlements in that country.

In the Collection it is said, that both in Kongo and Angola, the soil is in general fruitful, pro-

D   ducing

‖ J. Barbot, page 369.   † W. Smith, page 369.
‡ Bosman, page 403.

ducing great plenty of grain, Indian corn, and such quantities of rice, that it hardly bears any price, with fruit, roots, and palm oil in plenty.

The natives are generally a quiet people, who discover a good understanding, and behave in a friendly manner to strangers, being of a mild conversation, affable, and easily overcome with reason.

In the government of Kongo, the King appoints a judge in every particular division, to hear and determine disputes and civil causes; the judges imprison and release, or impose fines, according to the rule of custom; but in weighty matters, every one may appeal to the King, before whom all criminal causes are brought, in which he giveth sentence; but seldom condemneth to death.

The town of Leango stands in the midst of four Lordships, which abound in corn, fruit, &c. Here they make great quantities of cloth of divers kinds, very fine and curious; the inhabitants are seldom idle; they even make needle-work caps as they walk in the streets.

The slave trade is here principally managed by the Portugueze, who carry it far up into the inland countries. They are said to send off from these parts fifteen thousand slaves each year.

At Angola, about the 10th degree of South latitude, ends the trade for slaves.

CHAP.

CHAP. IV.

THE antienteſt accounts of the Negroes are from the Nubian Geography, and the writings of Leo the African. Some account of thoſe authors. The Arabians paſs into Guinea. The innocency and ſimplicity of the natives. They are ſubdued by the Moors. Heli Iſchai ſhakes off the Mooriſh yoke. The Portugueze make the firſt deſcent in Guinea, from whence they carry off ſome of the natives: More incurſions of the like kind. The Portugueze erect the firſt fort at D'Elwina: They begin the ſlave trade. Cada Moſto's teſtimony. Anderſon's account to the ſame purport. De la Caza's concern for the relief of the oppreſſed Indians: Goes over into Spain to plead their cauſe: His ſpeech before Charles the Fifth.

THE moſt antient account we have of the country of the Negroes, particularly that part ſituate on and between the two great rivers of Senegal and Gambia, is from the writings of two antient authors, one an Arabian, and the other a Moor. The firſt § wrote in Arabic, about the twelfth century. His works, printed in that language at Rome, were afterwards tranſlated into Latin, and printed at Paris, under the patronage of the famous Thuanus, chancellor of France, with the title of *Geographica Nubienſis*, containing

---

§ See Travels into different parts of Africa, by Francis Moor, with a letter to the publiſher.

containing an account of all the nations lying on the Senegal and Gambia. The other written by John Leo §, a Moor, born at Granada, in Spain, before the Moors were totally expelled from that kingdom. He resided in Africa; but being on a voyage from Tripoli to Tunis, was taken by some Italian Corsairs, who finding him possessed of several Arabian books, besides his own manuscripts, apprehended him to be a man of learning, and as such presented him to Pope Leo the Tenth. This Pope encouraging him, he embraced the Romish religion, and his description of Africa was published in Italian. From these writings we gather, that after the Mahometan religion had extended to the kingdom of Morocco, some of the promoters of it crossing the sandy deserts of Numidia, which separate that country from Guinea, found it inhabited by men, who, though under no regular government, and destitute of that knowledge the Arabians were favoured with, lived in content and peace. The first author particularly remarks, " That " they never made war, or travelled abroad, " but employed themselves in tending their " herds, or labouring in the ground." J. Leo says, page 65, " That they lived in common, " having no property in land, no tyrant nor su- " perior lord, but supported themselves in an " equal state, upon the natural produce of " the country, which afforded plenty of roots, " game, and honey. That ambition or avarice " never drove them into foreign countries to
" subdue

---

§ Ibid.

" subdue or cheat their neighbours. Thus they
" lived without toil or superfluities." " The
" antient inhabitants of Morocco, who wore
" coats of mail, and used swords and spears head-
" ed with iron, coming amongst those harmless
" and naked people, soon brought them under
" subjection, and divided that part of Guinea
" which lies on the rivers Senegal and Gambia
" into fifteen parts; those were the fifteen king-
" doms of the Negroes, over which the Moors
" presided, and the common people were Ne-
" groes. These Moors taught the Negroes the
" Mahometan religion, and arts of life; parti-
" cularly the use of iron, before unknown to
" them. About the 14th century, a native Ne-
" groe, called Heli Ischia, expelled the Moorish
" conquerors; but though the Negroes threw
" off the yoke of a foreign nation, they only
" changed a Libyan for a Negroe master. Heli
" Ischia himself becoming King, led the Negroes
" on to foreign wars, and established himself in
" power over a very large extent of country."
Since Leo's time, the Europeans have had very
little knowledge of those parts of Africa, nor do
they know what became of this great empire. It
is highly probable that it broke into pieces, and
that the natives again resumed many of their antient customs; for in the account published by
Francis Moor, in his travels on the river Gambia,
we find a mixture of the Moorish and Mahometan
customs, joined with the original simplicity
of the Negroes. It appears by accounts of antient
voyages, collected by Hackluit, Purchas, and
others, that it was about fifty years before the
discovery of America, that the Portugueze attempted

tempted to fail round Cape Bojador, which lies between their country and Guinea; this, after divers repulses occasioned by the violent currents, they effected; when landing on the western coasts of Africa, they soon began to make incursions into the country, and to seize and carry off the native inhabitants. As early as the year 1434, Alonzo Gonzales, the first who is recorded to have met with the natives, on that coast, pursued and attacked a number of them, when some were wounded, as was also one of the Portugueze; which the author records as the first blood spilt by Christians in those parts. Six years after, the same Gonzales again attacked the natives, and took twelve prisoners, with whom he returned to his vessels; he afterwards put a woman on shore, in order to induce the natives to redeem the prisoners; but the next day 150 of the inhabitants appeared on horses and camels provoking the Portugueze to land; which they not daring to venture, the natives discharged a volley of stones at them, and went off. After this, the Portugueze still continued to send vessels on the coast of Africa; particularly we read of their falling on a village, whence the inhabitants fled, and being pursued, twenty-five were taken: " *He that ran best,*" says the author, " *tak-*
" *ing the most.* In their way home they killed
" some of the natives, and took fifty-five more
" prisoners. * Afterwards Dinisanes Dagrama,
" with two other vessels, landed on the island of
" Arguin, where they took fifty-four Moors;
then

---

* Collection, vol. 1. page 13.

" then running along the coast eighty leagues
" farther, they at several times took fifty slaves;
" but here seven of the Portugueze were killed.
" Then being joined by several other vessels,
" Dinisanes proposed to destroy the island to re-
" venge the loss of the seven Portugueze; of
" which the Moors being apprized, fled, so that
" no more than twelve were found, whereof only
" four could be taken, the rest being killed, as
" also one of the Portugueze." Many more captures of this kind on the coast of Barbary and Guinea, are recorded to have been made in those early times by the Portugueze; who, in the year 1481, erected their first fort D'Elmina on that coast, from whence they soon opened a trade for slaves with the inland parts of Guinea.

From the foregoing accounts, it is undoubted, that the practice of making slaves of the Negroes, owes its origin to the early incursions of the Portugueze on the coast of Africa, solely from an inordinate desire of gain. This is clearly evidenced from their own historians, particularly *Cada Mosto*, about the year 1455, who writes†, " That before
" the trade was settled for purchasing slaves from
" the Moors at Arguin, sometimes four, and
" sometimes more Portugueze vessels, were
" used to come to that gulph, well armed; and
" landing by night, would surprize some fisher-
" men's villages; that they even entered into
" the country, and carried away Arabs of both
" sexes, whom they sold in Portugal." And also, " That the Portugueze and Spaniards,
" settled

---

† Collection, vol. 1. page 576.

"settled on four of the Canary islands, would go to the other island by night, and seize some of the natives of both sexes, whom they sent to be sold in Spain."

After the settlement of America, those devastations, and the captivating the miserable Africans, greatly increased.

Anderson, in his history of trade and commerce, at page 336, speaking of what passed in the year 1508, writes, " That the Spaniards had by this time found that the miserable Indian natives, whom they had made to work in their mines and fields, were not so robust and proper for those purposes as Negroes brought from Africa; wherefore they, about that time, began to import Negroes for that end in Hispaniola, from the Portugueze settlements on the Guinea coasts: and also afterwards for their sugar works." This oppression of the Indians had, even before this time, rouzed the zeal, as well as it did the compassion, of some of the truly pious of that day; particularly that of Bartholomew De las Casas, bishop of Chapia; whom a desire of being instrumental towards the conversion of the Indians, had invited into America. It is generally agreed by the writers of that age, that he was a man of perfect disinterestedness, and ardent charity; being affected with this sad spectacle, he returned to the court of Spain, and there made a true report of the matter; but not without being strongly opposed by those mercenary wretches, who had enslaved the Indians; yet being strong and indefatigable, he went to and fro between Europe and America, firmly determined

mined not to give over his purſuit but with his life. After long ſolicitation, and innumerable repulſes, he obtained leave to lay the matter before the Emperor Charles the Fifth, then King of Spain. As the contents of the ſpeech he made before the King in council, are very applicable to the caſe of the enſlaved Africans, and a lively evidence that the ſpirit of true piety ſpeaks the ſame language in the hearts of faithful men in all ages, for the relief of their fellow creatures from oppreſſion of every kind, I think it may not be improper here to tranſcribe the moſt intereſting parts of it. "I was," ſays this pious biſhop, "one of the firſt who went
" to America; neither curioſity nor intereſt
" prompted me to undertake ſo long and dan-
" gerous a voyage; the ſaving the ſouls of the
" heathen was my ſole object. Why was I not
" permitted, even at the expenſe of my blood,
" to ranſom ſo many thouſand ſouls, who fell
" unhappy victims to avarice or luſt? I have
" been an eye-witneſs to ſuch cruel treatment
" of the Indians, as is too horrid to be men-
" tioned at this time.—It is ſaid that barbarous
" executions were neceſſary to puniſh or check
" the rebellion of the Americans;——but to
" whom was this owing? Did not thoſe people
" receive the Spaniards, who firſt came amongſt
" them, with gentleneſs and humanity? Did
" they not ſhew more joy, in proportion, in
" laviſhing treaſure upon them, than the Spa-
" niards did greedineſs in receiving it? But
" our avarice was not yet ſatisfied;—though
" they gave up to us their land and their
" riches, we would tear from them their wives,
" their

" their children, and their liberties.——To
" blacken thefe unhappy people, their enemies
" affert, that they are fcarce human creatures;
" —but it is we that ought to blufh, for having
" been lefs men, and more barbarous, than
" they.—What right have we to enflave a peo-
" ple who are born free, and whom we dif-
" turbed, though they never offended us?—
" They are reprefented as a ftupid people, ad-
" dicted to vice;—but have they not contracted
" moft of their vices from the example of the
" Chriftians? And as to thofe vices peculiar to
" themfelves, have not the Chriftians quickly
" exceeded them therein? Neverthelefs it muft
" be granted, that the Indians ftill remain un-
" tainted with many vices ufual amongft the
" Europeans; fuch as ambition, blafphemy,
" treachery, and many like monfters, which
" have not yet took place with them; they have
" fcarce an idea of them; fo that in effect, all
" the advantage we can claim, is to have more
" elevated notions of things, and our natural
" faculties more unfolded and more cultivated
" than theirs.—Do not let us flatter our cor-
" ruptions, nor voluntarily blind ourfelves; *all
" nations are equally free*; one nation has no
" right to infringe upon the freedom of any
" other; let us do towards thefe people as we
" would have them to have done towards us,
" if they had landed upon our fhore, with the
" fame fuperiority of ftrength. And indeed,
" why fhould not things be equal on both fides?
" How long has the right of the ftrongeft been
" allowed to be the balance of juftice? What
" part of the gofpel gives a fanction to fuch a
                              " doctrine?

" doctrine? In what part of the whole earth did
" the apoſtles and the firſt promulgators of the
" goſpel ever claim a right over the lives, the
" freedom, or the ſubſtance of the Gentiles?
" What a ſtrange method this is of propagating
" the goſpel, that holy law of grace, which, from
" being ſlaves to Satan, initiates us into the
" freedom of the children of God.——Will it
" be poſſible for us to inſpire them with a love to
" its dictates, while they are ſo exaſperated at
" being diſpoſſeſſed of that invaluable bleſſing
" *Liberty?* The apoſtles ſubmitted to chains
" themſelves, but loaded no man with them.
" Chriſt came to free, not to enſlave us.—Sub-
" miſſion to the faith he left us, ought to be a
" voluntary act, and ſhould be propagated by
" perſuaſion, gentleneſs, and reaſon."

" At my firſt arrival in Hiſpaniola, (added
" the biſhop) it contained a million of inhabi-
" tants; and now (viz. in the ſpace of about
" twenty years) there remains ſcarce the hun-
" dredth part of them; thouſands have periſhed
" through want, fatigue, mercileſs puniſhment,
" cruelty, and barbarity. If the blood of *one*
" man unjuſtly ſhed, calls loudly for vengeance,
" how ſtrong muſt be the cry of that of *many*
" unhappy creatures which is ſhedding daily?"—
The good biſhop concluded his ſpeech, with im-
ploring the King's clemency for ſubjects ſo unjuſtly oppreſſed; and bravely declared, that heaven would one day call him to an account,
for the numberleſs acts of cruelty which he might
have prevented. The King applauded the biſhop's

shop's zeal; promised to second it; but so many of the great ones had an interest in continuing the oppression, that nothing was done; so that all the Indians in Hispaniola, except a few who had hid themselves in the most inaccessible mountains, were destroyed.

CHAP.

CHAP. V.

FIRST account of the English trading to Guinea. Thomas Windham and several others go to that coast. Some of the Negroes carried off by the English. Queen Elizabeth's charge to Captain Hawkins respecting the natives: Neverthelefs he goes on the coast, and carries off some of the Negroes. Patents are granted. The King of France objects to the Negroes being kept in slavery: As do the college of Cardinals at Rome. The natives, an inoffensive people; corrupted by the Europeans. The sentiments of the natives concerning the slave trade, from William Smith: Confirmed by Andrew Brew and James Barbot.

IT was about the year 1551, towards the latter end of the reign of King Edward the Sixth, when some London merchants sent out the first English ship, on a trading voyage to the coast of Guinea; this was soon followed by several others to the same parts; but the English not having then any plantations in the West Indies, and consequently no occasion for Negroes, such ships traded only for gold, elephant's teeth, and Guinea pepper. This trade was carried on at the hazard of losing their ships and cargoes, if they had fallen into the hands of the Portugueze, who claimed an exclusive right of trade, on account of the several settlements they had made

there

there†. In the year 1553, we find Captain Thomas Windham trading along the coast with 140 men, in three ships, and sailing as far as Benin, which lies about 3000 miles down the coast, to take in a load of pepper.§ Next year John Lock traded along the coast of Guinea, as far as D'Elmina, when he brought away considerable quantities of gold and ivory. He speaks well of the natives, and says,‡ *" That whoever " will deal with them must behave civilly, for they " will not traffic if ill used."* In 1555, William Towerson traded in a peaceable manner with the natives, who made complaint to him of the Portugueze, who were then settled in their castle at D'Elmina, saying, " *They were bad men, who* " *made them slaves if they could take them, putting* " *irons on their legs.*"

This bad example of the Portugueze was soon followed by some evil disposed Englishmen; for the same Captain Towerson relates, " ‖ That in " the course of his voyage, he perceived the " natives, near D'Elmina, unwilling to come to " him, and that he was at last attacked by them; " which he understood was done in revenge for " the wrong done them the year before, by one " Captain Gainsh, who had taken away the Ne- " groe Captain's son, and three others, with " their gold, &c. This caused them to join the " Portugueze, notwithstanding their hatred of
" them

---

† Astley's Collection, vol. 1. page 139.
§ Collection, vol. 1. p. 148.
‡ Ibid. 257.
‖ Ibid. 148.

"them against the English." The next year Captain Towerson brought these men back again; whereupon the Negroes shewed him much kindness†. Quickly after this, another instance of the same kind occurred, in the case of Captain George Fenner, who being on the coast, with three vessels, was also attacked by the Negroes, who wounded several of his people, and violently carried three of his men to their town. The Captain sent a messenger, offering any thing they desired for the ransom of his men; but they refused to deliver them, letting him know, "*That three weeks before, an English ship, which* "*came in the road, had carried off three of their* "*people; and that till they were brought again, they* "*they would not restore his men, even though they* "*should give their three ships to release them.*" It was probable the evil conduct of these, and some other Englishmen, was the occasion of what is mentioned in Hill's Naval History, viz. "That "when Captain Hawkins returned from his first "voyage to Africa, Queen Elizabeth sent for "him, when she expressed her concern, lest any "of the African Negroes should be carried off "without their free consent; which she declared "would be detestable, and would call down the "vengeance of heaven upon the undertakers." Hawkins made great promises, which nevertheless he did not perform; for his next voyage to the coast appears to have been principally calculated to procure Negroe slaves, in order to sell them to the Spaniards in the West Indies; which occasioned

---

† Collection, vol. 1. page 157.

occasioned the same author to use these remarkable words: "*Here began the horrid practice of forcing the Africans into slavery: an injustice and barbarity, which, so sure as there is vengeance in heaven for the worst of crimes, will some time be the destruction of all who act or who encourage it.*" This Captain Hawkins, afterwards Sir John Hawkins, seems to have been the first Englishman who gave public countenance to this wicked traffick: For Anderson, before mentioned, at page 401, says, "That in the year 1562, "Captain Hawkins, assisted by subscription of "sundry gentlemen, now fitted out three ships; "and having learnt that Negroes were a very "good commodity in Hispaniola, he sailed to "the coast of Guinea, took in Negroes, and "sailed with them for Hispaniola, where he "sold them, and his English commodities, and "loaded his three vessels with hides, sugar "and ginger, &c. with which he returned home "anno 1563, making a prosperous voyage." As it proved a lucrative business, the trade was continued both by Hawkins and others, as appears from the Naval Chronicle, page 55, where it is said, "That on the 18th of October, 1564, "Captain John Hawkins, with two ships of 700 "and 140 tons, sailed for Africa; that on the "8th of December they anchored to the South of "Cape Verd, where the Captain manned the "boat, and sent eighty men in armour into the "country, to see if they could take some Negroes; but the natives flying from them, they "returned to their ships, and proceeded farther "down the coast. Here they staid certain days, "sending their men ashore, in order (as the

author

" author fays) to burn and fpoil their towns
" and take the inhabitants. The land they
" obferved to be well cultivated, there being
" plenty of grain, and fruit of feveral forts,
" and the towns prettily laid out. On the 25th,
" being informed by the Portugueze of a town
" of Negroes called Bymba, where there was
" not only a quantity of gold, but an hundred
" and forty inhabitants, they refolved to attack
" it, having the Portugueze for their guide;
" but by mifmanagement they took but ten Ne-
" groes, having feven of their own men killed,
" and twenty-feven wounded. They then went
" farther down the coaft; when, having procured
" a number of Negroes, they proceeded to the
" Weft-Indies, where they fold them to the
" Spaniards." And in the fame Naval Chronicle,
at page 76, it is faid, " That in the year 1567,
" Francis Drake, before performing his voyage
" round the world, went with Sir John Haw-
" kins in his expedition to the coaft of Guinea;
" where taking in a cargo of flaves, they deter-
" mined to fteer for the Caribbee iflands." How
Queen Elizabeth fuffered fo grievous an in-
fringement of the rights of mankind to be perpetrated by her fubjects, and how fhe was perfuaded, about the 30th year of her reign, to
grant patents for carrying on a trade from the
North part of the river Senegal, to an hundred
leagues beyond Sierra Leona, which gave rife to
the prefent African company, is hard to account
for; any otherwife than that it arofe from the
mifreprefentation made to her of the fituation
of the Negroes, and of the advantages it was
pretended they would reap from being made

acquainted with the Christian religion. This was the case of Lewis the XIIIth, King of France, who, Labat, in his account of the isles of America, tells us, " Was extremely uneasy "at a law by which the Negroes of his colo- "nies were to be made slaves; but it being "strongly urged to him as the readiest means "for their conversion to Christianity, he ac- "quiesced therewith." Nevertheless, some of the Christian powers did not so easily give way in this matter; for we find *, " That Cardinal " Cibo, one of the Pope's principal ministers " of state, wrote a letter on behalf of the col- " lege of Cardinals, or great council at Rome, " to the missionaries in Congo, complaining " that the pernicious and abominable abuse of " selling slaves was yet continued, requiring " them to remedy the same, if possible; but " this the missionaries saw little hopes of ac- " complishing, by reason that the trade of the " country lay wholly in slaves and ivory."

From the foregoing accounts, as well as other authentic publications of this kind, it appears that it was the unwarrantable lust of gain, which first stimulated the Portugueze, and afterwards other Europeans, to engage in this horrid traffic. By the most authentic relations of those early times, the natives were an inoffensive people, who, when civilly used, traded amicably with the Europeans. It is recorded of those of Benin, the largest kingdom in Guinea †, *That they were a gentle, loving people*; and

Reynold

---

* Collection, vol. iii. page 164.
† Idem, vol. i. p. 202.

Reynold says †, *" They found more sincere proofs " of love and good will from the natives, than they " could find from the Spaniards and Portugueze, " even though they had relieved them from the greatest " misery."* And from the same relations there is no reason to think otherwise, but that they generally lived in peace amongst themselves; for I do not find, in the numerous publications I have perused on this subject, relating to these early times, of there being wars on that coast, nor of any sale of captives taken in battle, who would have been otherwise sacrificed by the victors ‡: notwithstanding some modern authors, in their publications relating to the West Indies, desirous of throwing a veil over the iniquity of the slave trade, have been hardy enough, upon mere supposition or report, to assert the contrary.

It was long after the Portugueze had made a practice of violently forcing the natives of Africa into slavery, that we read of the different Negroe nations making war upon each other, and selling their

---

† Collection, vol. 1. page 245.

‡ Note, this plea falls of itself, for if the Negroes apprehended they should be cruelly put to death, if they were not sent away, why do they manifest such reluctance and dread as they generally do, at being brought from their native country? William Smith, at page 28, says, *" The " Gambians abhor slavery, and will attempt any thing, though " never so desperate, to avoid it,"* and Thomas Philips, in his account of a voyage he performed to the coast of Guinea, writes, *" They, the Negroes, are so loth to leave their own country, " that they have often leaped out of the canoe, boat, or ship, " into the sea, and kept under water till they were drowned, " to avoid being taken up."*

their captives. And probably this was not the cafe, till thofe bordering on the coaft, who had been ufed to fupply the veffels with neceffaries, had become corrupted by their intercourfe with the Europeans, and were excited by drunkennefs and avarice to join them in carrying on thofe wicked fchemes, by which thofe unnatural wars were perpetrated; the inhabitants kept in continual alarms; the country laid wafte; and, as Francis Moor expreffes it, "Infinite numbers "fold into flavery." But that the Europeans "are the principal caufe of thefe devaftations, is particularly evidenced by one, whofe connexion with the trade would rather induce him to reprefent it in the faireft colours, to wit, William Smith, the perfon fent in the year 1726 by the African company to furvey their fettlements, who from the information he received of one of the factors, who had refided ten years in that country, says†, "That the dif- "cerning natives account it their greateft unhappi- "nefs, that they were ever vifited by the Europeans."
——"That we Chriftians introduced the traffic of "flaves; and that before our coming they lived in "peace."

In the accounts relating to the African trade, we find this melancholy truth farther afferted by fome of the principal directors in the different factories; particularly A. Brue says§, "That the "Europeans were far from defiring to act as peace- "makers amongft the Negroes; which would be
"acting

---

† William Smith, page 266.
§ Collection, vol. 2. page 98.

" *acting contrary to their interest, since the greater
" *the wars, the more slaves were procured.*" And
William Bosman also remarks[*], " That one of
" the former commanders *gave large sums of
" money to the Negroes of one nation, to induce them
" to attack some of the neighbouring nations, which
" occasioned a battle which was more bloody than the
" wars of Negroes usually are.*" This is confirmed
by J. Barbot, who says, " *That the country of
" D'Elmina, which was formerly very powerful and
" populous, was in his time so much drained of its
" inhabitants by the intestine wars fomented amongst
" the Negroes by the Dutch, that there did not re-
" main inhabitants enough to till the country.*"

---

[*] Bosman, page 31.

CHAP. VI.

THE conduct of the Europeans and Africans compared. Slavery more tolerable amongst the antients than in our colonies. As Christianity prevailed amongst the barbarous nations, the inconsistency of slavery became more apparent. The charters of manumission, granted in the early times of Christianity, founded on an apprehension of duty to God. The antient Britons, and other European nations, in their original state, no less barbarous than the Negroes. Slaves in Guinea used with much greater lenity than the Negroes are in the colonies.—Note. How the slaves are treated in Algiers, as also in Turkey.

SUCH is the woeful corruption of human nature, that every practice which flatters our pride and covetousness, will find its advocates! This is manifestly the case in the matter before us; the savageness of the Negroes in some of their customs, and particularly their deviating so far from the feelings of humanity, as to join in captivating and selling each other, gives their interested oppressors a pretence for representing them as unworthy of liberty, and the natural rights of mankind. But these sophisters turn the argument full upon themselves, when they instigate the poor creatures to such shocking impiety, by every means that fantastic subtilty can suggest; thereby shewing in their own conduct,

a more

a more glaring proof of the same depravity, and, if there was any reason in the argument, a greater unfitness for the same precious enjoyment. For though some of the ignorant Africans may be thus corrupted by their intercourse with the baser of the Europeon natives, and the use of strong liquors, this is no excuse for high-professing Christians, bred in a civilized country, with so many advantages unknown to the Africans, and pretending a superior degree of gospel light. Nor can it justify them in raising up fortunes to themselves from the misery of others, and calmly projecting voyages for the seizure of men naturally as free as themselves; and who they know are no otherwise to be procured than by such barbarous means, as none but those hardened wretches, who are lost to every sense of Christian compassion, can make use of. Let us diligently compare, and impartially weigh, the situation of those ignorant Negroes, and these enlightened Christians; then lift up the scale and say, which of the two are the greater savages.

Slavery has been for a long time in practice in many parts of Asia; it was also in usage among the Romans when that empire flourished; but, except in some particular instances, it was rather a reasonable servitude, no ways comparable to the unreasonable and unnatural service extorted from the Negroes in our colonies. A late learned author*, speaking of those times which succeeded the dissolution of that empire, acquaints us, that as Christianity prevailed, it very much removed

---

* See Robertson's History of Charles the 5th.

removed those wrong prejudices and practices, which had taken root in darker times: after the irruption of the Northern nations, and the introduction of the feudal or military government, whereby the most extensive power was lodged in a few members of society, to the depression of the rest, the common people were little better than slaves, and many were indeed such; but as Christianity gained ground, the gentle spirit of that religion, together with the doctrines it teaches, concerning the original equality of mankind, as well as the impartial eye with which the Almighty regards men of every condition, and admits them to a participation of his benefits; so far manifested the inconsistency of slavery with Christianity, that to set their fellow Christians at liberty was deemed an act of piety, highly meritorious, and acceptable to God†.

Accordingly

---

† In the years 1315 and 1318, Louis X. and his brother Philip, Kings of France, issued ordinances, declaring, "That as all men were by nature free-born, and as their kingdom was called the kingdom of Franks, they determined that it should be so in reality, as well as in name; therefore they appointed that enfranchisements should be granted throughout the whole kingdom, upon just and reasonable conditions." "These edicts were carried into immediate execution within the royal domain."

"——In England, as the spirit of liberty gained ground, the very name and idea of personal servitude, without any formal interposition of the legislature to prohibit it, was totally abolished."

"The effects of such a remarkable change in the condition of so great a part of the people, could not fail of being considerable and extensive. The husbandman, master of his own industry, and secure of reaping for

"himself

Accordingly a great part of the charters granted for the manumiffion or freedom of flaves about that time, are granted *pro amore Dei, for the love of God, pro mercede animæ, to obtain mercy for the foul.* Manumiffion was frequently granted on death-beds, or by latter wills. As the minds of men are at that time awakened to fentiments of humanity and piety, thefe deeds proceeded from religious motives. The fame author remarks, That there are feveral forms of thofe manumiffions ftill extant, all of them founded *on religious confiderations, and in order to procure the favour of God.* Since that time, that practice of keeping of men in flavery gradually ceafed amongft Chriftians, till it was renewed in the cafe before us. And as the prevalency of the fpirit of Chriftianity caufed men to emerge from the darknefs they then lay under, in this refpect; fo it is much to be feared that fo great a deviation therefrom, by the encouragement given to the flavery of the

Negroes

" himfelf the fruits of his labour, became farmer of
" the fame field where he had formerly been compelled
" to toil for the benefit of another. The odious name of
" mafter and of flave, the moft mortifying and depreffing
" of all diftinctions to human nature, were abolifhed. New
" profpects opened, and new incitements to ingenuity and
" enterprife prefented themfelves, to thofe who were eman-
" cipated. The expectation of bettering their fortune, as
" well as that of raifing themfelves to a more honourable
" condition, concurred in calling forth their activity and
" genius; and a numerous clafs of men, who formerly
" had no political exiftence, and were employed merely as
" inftruments of labour, became ufeful citizens, and con-
" tributed towards augmenting the force or riches of the
" fociety. which adopted them as members." William Robertfon's Hiftory of Charles the 5th, vol. 1. p. 35.

Negroes in our colonies, if continued, will, by degrees, reduce those countries which support and encourage it, but more immediately those parts of America which are in the practice of it, to the ignorance and barbarity of the darkest ages.

If instead of making slaves of the Negroes, the nations who assume the name and character of Christians, would use their endeavours to make the nations of Africa acquainted with the nature of the Christian religion, to give them a better sense of the true use of the blessings of life, the more beneficial arts and customs would, by degrees, be introduced amongst them; this care probably would produce the same effect upon them, which it had on the inhabitants of Europe, formerly as savage and barbarous as the natives of Africa. Those cruel wars amongst the blacks would be likely to cease, and a fair and honourable commerce, in time, take place throughout that vast country. It was by these means that the inhabitants of Europe, though formerly a barbarous people, became civilized. Indeed the account Julius Cæsar gives of the ancient Britons in their state of ignorance, is not such as should make us proud of ourselves, or lead us to despise the unpolished nations of the earth; for he informs us that they lived in many respects like our Indians, "Being clad with skins, painting their bodies, &c." He also adds, "That they, bro-
" ther with brother, and parents with children,
" had wives in common." A greater barbarity than any heard of amongst the Negroes. Nor doth Tacitus give a more honourable account of the Germans, from whom the Saxons, our immediate

ate anceſtors, ſprung. The Danes who ſucceeded them (who may alſo be numbered among our progenitors) were full as bad, if not worſe.

It is uſual for people to advance as a palliation in favour of keeping the Negroes in bondage, that there are ſlaves in Guinea, and that thoſe amongſt us might be ſo in their own country; but let ſuch conſider the inconſiſtency of our giving any countenance to ſlavery, becauſe the Africans, whom we eſteem a barbarous and ſavage people, allow of it, and perhaps the more from our example. Had the profeſſors of Chriſtianity acted indeed as ſuch, they might have been inſtrumental to convince the Negroes of their error in this reſpect; but even this, when inquired into, will be to us an occaſion of bluſhing, if we are not hardened to every ſenſe of ſhame, rather than a *palliation* of our iniquitous conduct; as it will appear that the ſlavery endured in Guinea, and other parts of Africa, and in Aſia, * is by no means ſo grievous as

that

---

* In the Hiſtory of the Piratical States of Barbary, printed in 1750, *ſaid to be* written by a perſon who reſided at Algiers, in a public character, at page 265 the author ſays, " The world exclaims againſt the Algerines for their
" cruel treatment of their ſlaves, and their employing even
" tortures to convert them to Mahometiſm : but this is a
" vulgar error, artfully propagated for ſelfiſh views. So
" far are their ſlaves from being ill uſed, that they muſt
" have committed ſome very great fault to ſuffer any
" puniſhment. Neither are they forced to work beyond
" their ſtrength, but rather ſpared, leſt they ſhould fall
" ſick. Some are ſo pleaſed with their ſituation, that they
" will not purchaſe their ranſom, though they are able."
It is the ſame generally through the Mahometan countries,

except

that in our colonies. Francis Moor, speaking of the natives living on the river Gambia, † says, "That some of the Negroes have many "house slaves, which are their greatest glory; "that those slaves live so well and easy, that it "is sometimes a hard matter to know the slaves "from their masters or mistresses. And that "though in some parts of Africa they sell their
"slaves

except in some particular instances, as that of Muley Ishmael, late Emperor of Morocco, who being naturally barbarous, frequently used both his subjects and slaves with cruelty. Yet even under him the usage the slaves met with was, in general, much more tolerable than that of the Negroe slaves in the West Indies. Captain Braithwaite, an author of credit, who accompanied consul general Russel in a congratulatory ambassy to Muley Ishmael's successor, upon his accession to the throne, says, "The situation of the "Christian slaves in Morocco was not near so bad as repre- "sented.—That it was true they were kept at labour by "the late Emperor, but not harder than our daily labour- "ers go through.—Masters of ships were never obliged to "work, nor such as had but a small matter of money to "give the Alcaide.—When sick, they had a religious house "appointed for them to go to, where they were well at- "tended: and whatever money in charity was sent them "by their friends in Europe, was their own." Braithwaite's revolutions of Morocco.

Lady Montague, wife of the English ambassador at Constantinople, in her letters, vol. 3. page 20, writes, "I "know you expect I should say something particular of the "slaves; and you will imagine me half a Turk, when I do "not speak of it with the same horror other Christians have "done before me; but I cannot forbear applauding the "humanity of the Turks to these creatures; they are not "ill used; and their slavery, in my opinion, is no worse "than servitude all over the world. It is true they have "no wages, but they give them yearly cloaths to a higher "value than our salaries to our ordinary servants."

† F Moor, p. 30.

" slaves born in the family, yet on the river
" Gambia they think it a very wicked thing."
The author adds, "He never heard of but one
" that ever sold a family slave, except for such
" crimes as they would have been sold for if
" they had been free." And in Astley's Collection, speaking of the customs of the Negroes in that large extent of country further down the coast, particularly denominated the coast of Guinea, it is said, ‡ " They have not many
" slaves on the coast; none but the King or
" nobles are permitted to buy or sell any; so
" that they are allowed only what are necessary
" for their families, or tilling the ground."
The same author adds, " *That they generally use*
" *their slaves well, and seldom correct them.*"

---

‡ Collection, vol. 2. page 647.

CHAP. VII.

MONTESQUIEU's sentiments on slavery. Moderation enjoined by the Mosaic law in the punishment of offenders. Morgan Goodwyn's account of the contempt and grievous rigour exercised upon the Negroes in his time. Account from Jamaica, relating to the inhuman treatment of them there. Bad effects attendant on slave-keeping, as well to the masters as the slaves. Extracts from several laws relating to Negroes. Richard Baxter's sentiments on slave-keeping.

THAT celebrated civilian Montesquieu, in his treatise *on the spirit of laws*, on the article of slavery says, " *It is neither useful to the " master nor slave ; to the slave because he can do " nothing through principle (or virtue); to the " master, because he contracts with his slave all sorts " of bad habits, insensibly accustoms himself to " want all moral virtues ; becomes haughty, hasty, " hard-hearted, passionate, voluptuous, and cruel.* The lamentable truth of this assertion was quickly verified in the English plantations. When the practice of slave-keeping was introduced, it soon produced its natural effects; it reconciled men, of otherwise good dispositions, to the most hard and cruel measures. It quickly proved, what, under the law of Moses, was apprehended would be the consequence of unmerciful chastisements. Deut. xxv. 2. " *And it " shall*

"*shall be if the wicked man be worthy to be beaten,*
"*that the judge should cause him to lie down, and*
"*to be beaten before his face, according to his fault,*
"*by a certain number; forty stripes may be given*
"*him, and not exceed.*" And the reason rendered, is out of respect to human nature, viz.
"*Left he should exceed, and beat him above these*
"*with many stripes, then thy brother should seem*
"*vile unto thee.*" As this effect soon followed the cause, the cruelest measures were adopted, in order to make the most of the poor *wretches* labour; and, in the minds of the masters, such an idea was excited of inferiority, in the nature of these their unhappy fellow creatures, that they esteemed and treated them as beasts of burden: pretending to doubt, and some of them even presuming to deny, that the efficacy of the death of Christ extended to them. Which is particularly noted in a book, intitled, " The Negroes " and Indians Advocate," dedicated to the then Archbishop of Canterbury, written so long since as in the year 1680, by Morgan Godwyn, thought to be a clergyman of the church of England.
* The same spirit of sympathy and zeal which
stirred

---

* There is a principle which is pure, placed in the human mind, which in different places or ages hath had different names; it is, however, pure, and proceeds from God.— It is deep and inward, confined to no forms of religion, nor excluded from any, where the heart stands in perfect sincerity. In whomsoever this takes root and grows, of what nation soever, they become brethren in the best sense of the expression. Using ourselves to take ways which appear most easy to us, when inconsistent with that purity which is without beginning, we thereby set up a government of our own,
and

ftirred up the good Bifhop of Capia to plead
with fo much energy the kindred caufe of the
Indians

and deny obedience to Him whofe fervice is true liberty: He that has a fervant, made fo wrongfully, and knows it to be fo, when he treats him otherwife than a free man, when he reaps the benefit of his labour, without paying him fuch wages as are reafonably due to free men for the like fervice; thefe things, though done in calmnefs, without any fhew of diforder, do yet deprave the mind, in like manner, and with as great certainty, as prevailing cold congeals water. Thefe fteps taken by mafters, and their conduct ftriking the minds of their children, whilft young, leave lefs room for that which is good to work upon them. The cuftoms of their parents, their neighbours, and the people with whom they converfe, working upon their minds, and they from thence conceiving wrong ideas of things, and modes of conduct, the entrance into their hearts becomes in a great meafure fhut up againft the gentle movings of uncreated purity.

From one age to another the gloom grows thicker and darker, till error gets eftablifhed by general opinion; but whoever attends to perfect goodnefs, and remains under the melting influence of it, finds a path unknown to many, and fees the neceffity to lean upon the arm of divine ftrength, and dwell alone, or with a few in the right, committing their caufe to him who is a refuge to his people. Negroes are our fellow-creatures, and their prefent condition among us requires our ferious confideration. We know not the time, when thofe fcales, in which mountains are weighed, may turn. The Parent of mankind is gracious, his care is over his fmalleft creatures, and a multitude of men efcape not his notice; and though many of them are trodden down and defpifed, yet he remembers them. He feeth their affliction, and looketh upon the fpreading increafing exaltation of the oppreffor. He turns the channel of power, humbles the moft haughty people, and gives deliverance to the oppreffed, at fuch periods as are confiftent with his infinite juftice and goodnefs. And wherever gain is preferred to equity, and wrong things
publicly

Indians of America, an hundred and fifty years before, was equally operating about a century paſt on the minds of ſome of the well diſpoſed of that day; amongſt others this worthy clergyman, having been an eye-witneſs of the oppreſſion and cruelty exerciſed upon the Negroe and Indian ſlaves, endeavoured to raiſe the attention of thoſe, in whoſe power it might be to procure them relief; amongſt other matters, in his addreſs to the Archbiſhop, he remarks in ſubſtance, " That the people of the iſland of
" Barbadoes were not content with exerciſing
" the greateſt hardneſs and barbarity upon the
" Negroes, in making the moſt of their labour,
" without any regard to the calls of humanity,
" but that they had ſuffered ſuch a ſlight and
" undervaluement to prevail in their minds to-
" wards theſe their oppreſſed fellow-creatures,
" as to diſcourage any ſtep being taken, where-
" by they might be made acquainted with the
" Chriſtian religion. That their conduct to-
" wards their ſlaves was ſuch as gave him rea-
" ſon to believe, that either they had ſuffered
" a ſpirit of infidelity, a ſpirit quite contrary
" to the nature of the goſpel, to prevail in them,
" or that it muſt be their eſtabliſhed opinion,
" that the Negroes had no more ſouls than
" beaſts; that hence they concluded them to
" be neither ſuſceptible of religious impreſſions,

---

publicly encouraged, to that degree that wickedneſs takes root and ſpreads wide amongſt the inhabitants of a country, there is a real cauſe for ſorrow, to all ſuch whoſe love to mankind ſtands on a true principle, and wiſely conſider the end and event of things." Conſiderations on keeping Negroes, by John Woolman, part 2. p. 50.

" nor

" nor fit objects for the redeeming grace of God
" to operate upon. That under this perfuafion,
" and from a difpofition of cruelty, they treated
" them with far lefs humanity than they did
" their cattle; for, fays he, they do not ftarve
" their horfes, which they expect fhould both
" carry and credit them on the road; nor pinch
" the cow, by whofe milk they are fuftained;
" which yet, to their eternal fhame, is too fre-
" quently the lot and condition of thofe poor
" people, from whofe labour their wealth and
" livelihood doth wholly arife; not only in their
" diet, but in their cloathing, and overworking
" fome of them even to death, (which is parti-
" cularly the calamity of the moft innocent and
" laborious) but alfo in tormenting and whip-
" ping them almoft, and fometimes quite, to
" death, upon even fmall mifcarriages. He
" apprehends it was from this prejudice againft
" the Negroes, that arofe thofe fupercilious
" checks and frowns he frequently met with,
" when ufing innocent arguments and perfua-
" fions, in the way of his duty as a minifter of
" the gofpel, to labour for the convincement
" and converfion of the Negroes; being re-
" peatedly told, with fpiteful fcoffings, (even
" by fome efteemed religious) that the Negroes
" were no more fufceptible of receiving bene-
" fit, by becoming members of the church,
" than their dogs and bitches. The ufual an-
" fwer he received, when exhorting their mafters
" to do their duty in that refpect, being, *What!*
" *thefe black dogs be made Chriftians! What! they*
" *be made like us!* with abundance more of the
" fame. Neverthelefs, he remarks that the Ne-
" groes

" groes were capable, not only of being taught
" to read and write, &c. but divers of them
" eminent in the management of business. He
" declares them to have an equal right with
" us to the merits of Christ; of which if through
" neglect or avarice they are deprived, that
" judgment which was denounced against wicked
" Ahab, must befal us: *Our life shall go for*
" *theirs.* The loss of their souls will be required
" at our hands, to whom God hath given so
" blessed an opportunity of being instrumental
" to their salvation."

He complains, " That they were suffered to
" live with their women in no better way than
" direct fornication; no care being taken to
" oblige them to continue together when mar-
" ried; but that they were suffered at their will
" to leave their wives, and take to other wo-
" men." I shall conclude this sympathizing
clergyman's observations, with an instance he
gives, to shew, " that not only discouragements
" and scoffs at that time prevailed in Barbadoes,
" to establish an opinion that the Negroes were
" not capable of religious impressions, but that
" even violence and great abuses were used to
" prevent any thing of the kind taking place. It
" was in the case of a poor Negroe, who hav-
" ing, at his own request, prevailed on a clergy-
" man to administer baptism to him, on his
" return home the brutish overseer took him to
" task, giving him to understand, that that was
" no Sunday's work for those of his complexion;
" that he had other business for him, the neglect
" whereof should cost him an afternoon's bap-
" tism in blood, as he in the morning had re-
" ceived

"ceived a baptism with water, (these, says the
"clergyman, were his own words) which he
"accordingly made good; of which the Negroe
"complained to him, and he to the governor;
"nevertheless, the poor miserable creature was
"ever after so unmercifully treated by that in-
"human wretch, the overseer, that, to avoid his
"cruelty, betaking himself to the woods, he
"there perished." This instance is applicable to none but the cruel perpetrator; and yet it is an instance of what, in a greater or less degree, may frequently happen, when those poor wretches are left to the will of such brutish inconsiderate creatures as those overseers often are. This is confirmed in a *History of Jamaica*, written in thirteen letters, about the year 1740, by a person then residing in that island, who writes as follows: " I shall not now enter upon the ques-
"tion, whether the slavery of the Negroes be
"agreeable to the laws of nature or not; though
"it seems extremely hard they should be re-
"duced to serve and toil for the benefit of
"others, without the least advantage to them-
"selves. Happy Britannia, where slavery is
"never known! where liberty and freedom
"cheers every misfortune. Here," says the author, " we can boast of no such blessing; we
"have at least ten slaves to one freeman. I
"incline to touch the hardships which these
"poor creatures suffer, in the tenderest man-
"ner, from a particular regard which I have to
"many of their masters, but I cannot conceal
"their sad circumstances intirely: the most
"trivial error is punished with most terrible
"whipping. I have seen some of them treated
"in

" in that cruel manner, for no other reason but
" to satisfy the brutish pleasure of an overseer,
" who has their punishment mostly at his dis-
" cretion. I have seen their bodies all in a
" gore of blood, the skin torn off their backs
" with the cruel whip; beaten pepper and salt
" rubbed in the wounds, and a large stick of
" sealing-wax dropped leisurely upon them. It
" is no wonder, if the horrid pain of such in-
" human tortures incline them to rebel. Most
" of these slaves are brought from the coast of
" Guinea: when they first arrive, it is observ-
" ed, they are simple and very innocent crea-
" tures; but soon turn to be roguish enough:
" and when they come to be whipt, urge the
" example of the whites for an excuse of their
" faults."

These accounts of the deep depravity of mind attendant on the practice of slavery, verify the truth of Montesquieu's remark of its pernicious effects. And although the same degree of opposition to instructing the Negroes may not now appear in the islands as formerly, especially since the Society appointed for propagating the Gospel have possessed a number of Negroes in one of them; nevertheless the situation of these oppressed people is yet dreadful, as well to themselves, as in its consequence to their hard taskmasters, and their offspring; as must be evident to every impartial person who is acquainted with the treatment they generally receive, or with the laws which from time to time have been made in the colonies, with respect to the Negroes; some of them being absolutely inconsistent with reason, and shocking to humanity.

nity. By the 329th act of the assembly of Barbadoes, page 125, it is enacted, "That if any "Negroe or other slave under punishment by "his master, or his order, for running away, "or any other crime or misdemeanors towards "his said master, unfortunately shall suffer in "life or member, (which seldom happens) no "person whatsoever shall be liable to any fine "therefore. But if any man shall, *of wanton-* "*ness, or only of bloody-mindedness or cruel inten-* "*tion, wilfully kill a Negroe, or other slave of his* "*own, he shall pay into the public treasury, fifteen* "*pounds sterling.*" Now that the life of a man should be so lightly valued, as that fifteen pounds should be judged a sufficient indemnification of the murder of one, even when it is avowedly done *wilfully, wantonly, cruelly, or of bloody-mindedness,* is a tyranny hardly to be paralleled: nevertheless human laws cannot make void the righteous law of God, or prevent the inquisition of that awful judgment-day, when, "*at the hand of every man's brother the life of* "*man shall be required.*" By the law of South Carolina, the person that killeth a Negroe is only subject to a fine, or twelve months imprisonment: it is the same in most, if not all the West-Indies. And by an act of the assembly of Virginia, (4 Ann. Ch. 49. sect. 27. p. 227.) after proclamation is issued against slaves, "that run away and lie out, *it is lawful for* "*any person whatsoever to kill and destroy such* "*slaves, by such ways and means as he, she, or* "*they shall think fit, without accusation or im-* "*peachment of any crime for the same.*" And lest private interest should incline the planter to mercy,

mercy, it is provided, " *That every slave so killed, in pursuance of this act, shall be paid for by the public.*"

It was doubtless a like sense of sympathy with that expressed by Morgan Godwyn before-mentioned, for the oppressed Negroes, and like zeal for the cause of religion, so manifestly trampled upon in the case of the Negroes, which induced Richard Baxter, an eminent preacher amongst the Dissenters in the last century, in his *Christian Directory*, to express himself as follows, viz. " Do you mark how God hath followed you with plagues; and may not conscience tell you, that it is for your inhumanity to the souls and bodies of men?"—" To go as pirates, and catch up poor Negroes, or people of another land, that never forfeited life or liberty, and to make them slaves, and sell them, is one of the worst kinds of thievery in the world; and such persons are to be taken for the common enemies of mankind; and they that buy them and use them as beasts for their mere commodity, and betray, or destroy, or neglect their souls, are fitter to be called devils incarnate than Christians: it is an heinous sin to buy them, unless it be in charity to deliver them. Undoubtedly they are presently bound to deliver them, because by right the man is his own, therefore no man else can have a just title to him."

CHAP.

CHAP. VIII.

GRIFFITH HUGHES's Account of the number of Negroes in Barbadoes. Cannot keep up their usual number without a yearly recruit. Excessive hardships wear the Negroes down in a surprising manner. A servitude without a condition, inconsistent with reason and natural justice. The general usage the Negroes meet with in the West-Indies. Inhuman calculations of the strength and lives of the Negroes. Dreadful consequences which may be expected from the cruelty exercised upon this oppressed part of mankind.

WE are told by Griffith Hughes, rector of St. Lucy in Barbadoes, in his natural history of that island, printed in the year 1750, "That there were between sixty-five and seventy thousand Negroes, at that time, in the island, though formerly they had a greater number: that in order to keep up a necessary number, they were obliged to have a yearly supply from Africa: that the hard labour, and often want of necessaries, which these unhappy creatures are obliged to undergo, destroy a greater number than are bred there." He adds, " That the capacities of their minds, in the common affairs of life, are but little inferior, if at all, to those of the Europeans. If they fail in some arts, he says, it may be owing more to their want of education, and the depression of their spirits by slavery, than

" to any want of natural abilities." This deftruction of the human fpecies, through unnatural hardſhips, and want of neceſſary fupplies, in the cafe of the Negroes, is farther confirmed in *An Account of the European Settlements in America,* printed London, 1757, where it is faid, part 6. chap. 11th, " The Negroes in our co-
" lonies endure a flavery more complete, and
" attended with far worfe circumftances, than
" what any people in their condition fuffer in
" any other part of the world, or have fuffered
" in any other period of time: proofs of this
" are not wanting. The prodigious wafte which
" we experience in this unhappy part of our
" fpecies, is a full and melancholy evidence of
" this truth. The ifland of Barbadoes, (the
" Negroes upon which do not amount to eighty
" thoufand) notwithstanding all the means which
" they ufe to increafe them by propagation, and
" that the climate is in every refpect (except
" that of being more wholefome) exactly re-
" fembling the climate from whence they come;
" notwithftanding all this, Barbadoes lies under
" a neceffity of an annual recruit of five thou-
" fand flaves, to keep up the ftock at the num-
" ber I have mentioned. This prodigious fai-
" lure, which is at leaft in the fame proportion
" in all our iflands, fhews demonftratively that
" fome uncommon and unfupportable hardfhip
" lies upon the Negroes, which wears them
" down in fuch a furprifing manner."

In an account of part of North America, publiſhed by Thomas Jeffery, 1761, the author, fpeaking of the ufage the Negroes receive in the Weft-India iflands, fays, " It is impoffible for
" a human

" a human heart to reflect upon the servitude of
" these dregs of mankind, without in some
" measure feeling for their misery, which ends
" but with their lives.—Nothing can be more
" wretched than the condition of this people.
" One would imagine, they were framed to be
" the disgrace of the human species; banished
" from their country, and deprived of that bles-
" sing, liberty, on which all other nations set
" the greatest value, they are in a measure re-
" duced to the condition of beasts of burthen.
" In general, a few roots, potatoes especially,
" are their food, and two rags, which neither
" screen them from the heat of the day, nor the
" extraordinary coolness of the night, all their
" covering; their sleep very short; their labour
" almost continual: they receive no wages, but
" have twenty lashes for the smallest fault." *A
thoughtful* person, who had an opportunity of observing the miserable condition of the Negroes in one of our West-India islands, writes thus: " I met with daily exercise to see the
" treatment which those miserable wretches met
" with from their masters; with but few ex-
" ceptions. They whip them most unmerci-
" fully on small occasions: you will see their
" bodies all whealed and scarred; in short, they
" seem to set no other value on their lives, than
" as they cost them so much money; and are
" restrained from killing them, when angry, by
" no worthier consideration, than that they lose
" so much. They act as though they did not
" look upon them as a race of human creatures,
" who have reason, and remembrance of mis-
" fortunes, but as beasts; like oxen, who are
" stubborn,

"stubborn, hardy, and senseless, fit for burdens,
"and designed to bear them: they will not
"allow them to have any claim to human pri-
"vileges, or scarce indeed to be regarded as the
"work of God. Though it was consistent
"with the justice of our Maker to pronounce
"the sentence on our common parent, and
"through him to all succeeding generations,
"*That he and they should eat their bread by the
"sweat of their brows*; yet does it not stand re-
"corded by the same eternal truth, *That the
"labourer is worthy of his hire?* It cannot
"be allowed, in natural justice, that there
"should be a servitude without condition;
"a cruel, endless servitude. It cannot be re-
"concileable to natural justice, that whole na-
"tions, nay, whole continents of men, should
"be devoted to do the drudgery of life for
"others, be dragged away from their attach-
"ments of relations and societies, and be made
"to serve the appetites and pleasure of a race
"of men, whose superiority has been obtained
"by illegal force."

Sir Hans Sloane, in the introduction to his natural history of Jamaica, in the account he gives of the treatment the Negroes met with there, speaking of the punishments inflicted on them, says, page 56, " For rebellion, the pu-
"nishment is burning them, by nailing them
"down to the ground with crooked sticks on
"every limb, and then applying the fire, by
"degrees, from the feet and hands, burning
"them gradually up to the head, whereby
"*their pains are extravagant.* For crimes of a
"less nature, gelding or chopping off half the
"foot

"foot with an axe.——" For negligence, they
" are ufually whipped by the overfeers with
" lance-wood fwitches.——After they are whip-
" ped till they are raw, fome put on their fkins
" pepper and falt, to make them fmart; at
" other times, their mafters will drop melted
" wax on their fkins, and ufe feveral *very exqui-*
" *fite torments.*" In that ifland, the owners of
the Negroe flaves fet afide to each a parcel of
ground, and allow them half a day at the latter
end of the week, which, with the day appointed
by the divine injunction to be a day of reft and
fervice to God, and which ought to be kept as
fuch, is the only time allowed them to manure
their ground. This, with a few herrings, or
other falt fifh, is what is given for their fupport.
Their allowance for cloathing in the ifland, is
feldom more than fix yards of oznabrigs each
year. And in the more northern colonies,
where the piercing wefterly winds are long and
fenfibly felt, thefe poor Africans fuffer much
for want of fufficient cloathing; indeed fome
have none till they are able to pay for it
by their labour. The time that the Negroes
work in the Weft Indies, is from day-break
till noon; then again from two o'clock till
dark (during which time, they are attended by
overfeers, who feverely fcourge thofe who appear
to them dilatory); and before they are fuffered to go to their quarters, they have ftill
fomething to do, as collecting the herbage for
the horfes, gathering fuel for the boilers, &c.
fo that it is often paft twelve before they can
get home, when they have fcarce time to grind
and boil their Indian corn; whereby, if their
food

food was not prepared the evening before, it sometimes happens that they are called again to labour before they can satisfy their hunger. And here no excuse or delay will avail; for if they are not in the field immediately upon the usual notice, they must expect to feel the overseer's lash. In crop time (which lasts many months) they are obliged, by turns, to work most of the night in the boiling house. Thus their owners, from a desire to make the greatest gain by the labour of their slaves, lay heavy burthens on them, and yet feed and cloath them very sparingly, and some scarce feed or cloath them at all; so that the poor creatures are obliged to shift for their living in the best manner they can, which occasions their being often killed in the neighbouring lands, stealing potatoes, or other food, to satisfy their hunger. And if they take any thing from the plantation they belong to, though under such pressing want, their owners will correct them severely for taking a little of what they have so hardly laboured for; whilst many of themselves riot in the greatest luxury and excess. It is matter of astonishment how a people, who as a nation, are looked upon as generous and humane, and so much value themselves for their uncommon sense of the benefit of liberty, can live in the practice of such extreme oppression and inhumanity, without seeing the inconsistency of such conduct, and feeling great remorse. Nor is it less amazing to hear these men calmly making calculations about the strength and lives of their fellow men. In Jamaica, if six in ten of the new imported Negroes survive the seasoning, it is looked upon as a

gaining

gaining purchase. And in most of the other plantations, if the Negroes live eight or nine years, their labour is reckoned a sufficient compensation for their cost. If calculations of this sort were made on the strength and labour of beasts of burden, it would not appear so strange; but even then, a merciful man would certainly use his beast with more mercy than is usually shewn to the poor Negroes. Will not the groans, the dying groans, of this deeply afflicted and oppressed people reach heaven? and when the cup of iniquity is full, must not the inevitable consequence be, the pouring forth the judgments of God upon the oppressors? But alas! is it not too manifest that this oppression has already long been the object of the divine displeasure? For what heavier judgment, what greater calamity, can befall any people, than to become subject to that hardness of heart, that forgetfulness of God, and insensibility to every religious impression, as well as that general depravation of manners, which so much prevails in these colonies, in proportion as they have more or less enriched themselves at the expence of the blood and bondage of the Negroes.

It is a dreadful consideration, as a late author remarks, that out of the stock of eighty thousand Negroes in Barbadoes, there die every year five thousand more than are born in that island; which failure is probably in the same proportion in the other islands. *In effect, this people is under a necessity of being entirely renewed every sixteen years.* And what must we think of the management of a people, who, far from increasing greatly, as those who have no loss by

war

war ought to do, muſt, in ſo ſhort a time as ſixteen years, without foreign recruits, be entirely conſumed to a man! Is it not a Chriſtian doctrine, *that the labourer is worthy of his hire?* And hath not the Lord, by the mouth of his prophet, pronounced, " *Wo. unto that man who buildeth* " *his houſe by unrighteouſneſs, and his chambers by* " *wrong; who uſes his neighbour's ſervice without* " *wages, and giveth him nought for his work?*" And yet the poor Negroe ſlaves are conſtrained, like the beaſts, by beating, to work hard without hire or recompence, and receive nothing from the hand of their unmerciful maſters, but ſuch a wretched proviſion as will ſcarce ſupport them under their fatigues. The intolerable hardſhips many of the ſlaves undergo, are ſufficiently proved by the ſhortneſs of their lives.— And who are theſe miſerable creatures, that receive ſuch barbarous treatment from the planter? Can we reſtrain our juſt indignation, when we conſider that they are undoubtedly *his brethren! his neighbours! the children of the ſame Father, and ſome of thoſe for whom Chriſt died, as truly as for the planter himſelf.* Let the opulent planter, or merchant, prove that his Negroe ſlave is not his brother, or that he is not his neighbour, in the ſcripture ſenſe of theſe appellations; and if he is not able ſo to do, how will he juſtify the buying and ſelling of his brethren, as if they were of no more conſideration than his cattle? The wearing them out with continual labour, before they have lived out half their days? The ſevere whipping and torturing them, even to death, if they reſiſt his inſupportable tyranny? Let the hardieſt ſlave-holder look forward to the tremendous day,

day, when he must give an account to God of his stewardship; and let him seriously consider whether, at such a time, he thinks he shall be able to satisfy himself, that any act of buying and selling, or the fate of war, or the birth of children in his house, plantation, or territories, or any other circumstance whatever, can give him such an absolute property in the persons of men, as will justify his retaining them as slaves, and treating them as beasts? Let him diligently consider whether there will not always remain to the slave a *superior* property or right to the fruit of his own labour; and more especially to his own person; that being which was given him by God, and which none but the Giver can justly claim?

CHAP. IX.

THE advantage which would have accrued to the natives of Guinea, if the Europeans had acted towards them agreeably to the dictates of humanity and Chriſtianity. *An inordinate* deſire of gain in the Europeans, the true occaſion of the ſlave trade. Notice of the miſrepreſentations of the Negroes by moſt authors, in order to palliate the iniquity of the ſlave trade. Thoſe miſrepreſentations refuted, particularly with reſpect *to the Hottentot Negroes.*

FROM the foregoing accounts of the natural diſpoſition of the Negroes, and the fruitfulneſs of moſt parts of Guinea, which are confirmed by authors of candour, who have written from their own knowledge, it may well be concluded, that the Negroes acquaintance with the Europeans might have been a happineſs to them, if theſe laſt had not only borne the name, but had alſo acted the part, of Chriſtians, and uſed their endeavours by example, as well as precept, to make them acquainted with the glad tidings of the goſpel, which breathes peace and good will to man, and with that change of heart, that redemption from ſin, which Chriſtianity propoſeth. Innocence and love might then have prevailed, and nothing would have been wanting to complete the happineſs of the ſimple Africans. But the reverſe has happened; the Europeans, forgetful of their duty as men and Chriſtians, have

have conducted themselves in so iniquitous a manner, as must necessarily raise in the minds of the thoughtful and well-disposed Negroes, the utmost scorn and detestation of the very name of Christians. All other considerations have given way to an insatiable desire of gain, which has been the principal and moving cause of the most *iniquitous and dreadful scene* that was, perhaps, ever acted upon the face of the earth. Instead of making use of that superior knowledge with which the Almighty, the common Parent of mankind, had favoured them, to strengthen the principle of peace and good will in the breasts of the incautious Negroes, the Europeans have, by their bad example, led them into excess of drunkenness, debauchery, and avarice; whereby every passion of corrupt nature being inflamed, they have been easily prevailed upon to make war, and captivate one another; as well to furnish means for the excesses they had been habituated to, as to satisfy the greedy desire of gain in their profligate employers, who to this intent have furnished them with prodigious quantities of arms and ammunition. Thus they have been hurried into confusion, distress, and all the extremities of temporal misery; every thing, even the power of their kings, has been made subservient to this wicked purpose; for instead of being protectors of their subjects, some of those rulers, corrupted by the excessive love of spirituous liquors, and the tempting baits laid before them by the factors, have invaded the liberties of their unhappy subjects, and are become their oppressors.

Here

Here it may be neceſſary to obſerve, that the accounts we have of the inhabitants of Guinea, are chiefly given by perſons engaged in the trade, who, from ſelf-intereſted views, have deſcribed them in ſuch colours as were leaſt likely to excite compaſſion and reſpect, and endeavoured to reconcile ſo manifeſt a violation of the rights of mankind to the minds of the purchaſers; yet they cannot but allow the Negroes to be poſſeſſed of ſome good qualities, though they contrive as much as poſſible to caſt a ſhade over them. A particular inſtance of this appears in Aſtley's Collection, vol. ii. p. 73. where the author, ſpeaking of the Mandingos ſettled at Galem, which is ſituated 900 miles up the Senegal, after ſaying that they carry on a commerce to all the neighbouring kingdoms, and amaſs riches, adds, " That excepting *the vices peculiar to the Blacks,* " they are a good ſort of people, honeſt, hoſpi-" table, juſt to their word, laborious, induſ-" trious, and very ready to learn arts and ſci-" ences." Here it is difficult to imagine what vices can be peculiarly attendant on a people ſo well diſpoſed as the author deſcribes theſe to be. With reſpect to the charge ſome authors have brought againſt them, as being void of all natural affection, it is frequently contradicted by others. In vol. ii. of the Collection, p. 275, and 629, the Negroes of North Guinea, and the Gold Coaſt, are ſaid *to be fond of their children, whom they love with tenderneſs.* And Boſman ſays, p. 340, " Not a few in his country (viz. Holland) " fondly imagine, that parents here ſell their " children, men their wives, and one brother " the other: but thoſe who think ſo deceive
" them-

" themselves; for this never happens on any
" other account but that of necessity, or some
" great crime." The same is repeated by J.
Barbot, p. 326, and also confirmed by Sir Hans
Sloane, in the introduction to his natural history
of Jamaica; where speaking of the Negroes, he
says, " They are usually thought to be haters
" of their own children, and therefore it is be-
" lieved that they sell and dispose of them to
" strangers for money: but this is not true;
" for the Negroes of Guinea being divided into
" several captainships, as well as the Indians of
" America, have wars; and besides those slain in
" battle, many prisoners are taken, who are sold
" for slaves, and brought hither: but the pa-
" rents here, although their children are slaves
" for ever, yet have so great love for them, that
" no master dares sell, or give away, one of their
" little ones, unless they care not whether their
" parents hang themselves or no." J. Barbot,
speaking of the occasion of the natives of Guinea
being represented as a treacherous people, ascribes
it to the Hollanders (and doubtless other Europeans) usurping authority, and fomenting divisions between the Negroes. At page 110, he
says, " It is well known that many of the Eu-
" ropean nations trading amongst those people,
" have very unjustly and inhumanly, without
" any provocation, stolen away, from time to
" time, abundance of the people, not only on
" this coast, but almost every where in Guinea,
" who have come on board their ships in a
" harmless and confiding manner: these they
" have in great numbers carried away, and sold
" in the plantations, with other slaves which
" they

"they had purchased." And although some of the Negroes may be justly charged with indolence and supineness, yet many others are frequently mentioned by authors *as a careful, industrious, and even laborious* people. But nothing shews more clearly how unsafe it is to form a judgment of distant people from the accounts given of them by travellers, who have taken but a transient view of things, than the case of the Hottentots, viz. those several nations of Negroes who inhabit the most southern part of Africa: *these people* are represented by several authors, who appear to have very much copied their relations one from the other, as so savage and barbarous as to have little of human, but the shape: but these accounts are strongly contradicted by others, particularly Peter Kolben, who has given a circumstantial relation of the disposition and manners of those people. * He was a man of learning, sent from the court of Prussia solely to make astronomical and natural observations there; and having no interest in the slavery of the Negroes, had not the same inducement as most other relators had, to misrepresent the natives of Africa. He resided eight years at and about the Cape of Good Hope, during which time he examined with great care into the customs, manners, and the opinions of the Hottentots, whence he sets these people in a quite different light from what they appear in former authors, whom he corrects, and blames for the falsehoods they have wantonly told

---

* See Kolben's account of the Cape of Good Hope.

told of them. At p. 61, he fays, " The details
" we have in feveral authors, are for the moft
" part made up of inventions and hearfays,
" which generally prove falfe." Neverthelefs,
he allows they are juftly to be blamed for their
floth.—*The love of liberty and indolence is their all:
compulfion is death to them. While neceffity obliges
them to work they are very tractable, obedient, and
faithful; but when they have got enough to fatisfy
the prefent want, they are deaf to all further en-
treaty.* He alfo cenfures them for their naftinefs,
the effect of floth; and for their love of drink,
and the practice of fome unnatural cuftoms,
which long ufe has eftablifhed amongft them;
which, neverthelefs, from the general good difpofition of thefe people, there is great reafon to
believe they might be perfuaded to refrain from,
if a truly Chriftian care had been extended towards them. He fays, " They are eminently
" diftinguifhed by many virtues, as their mutual
" benevolence, friendfhip, and hofpitality; they
" breathe kindnefs and good-will to one ano-
" ther, and feek all opportunities of obliging.
" Is a Hottentot's affiftance required by one of
" his countrymen? he runs to give it. Is his
" advice afked? he gives it with fincerity. Is
" his countryman in want? he relieves him to
" the utmoft of his power." Their hofpitality
extends even to European ftrangers: in travel-
ling through the Cape countries, you meet with
a chearful and open reception, in whatfoever village you come to. In fhort, he fays, p. 339,
" The integrity of the Hottentots, their ftrict-
" nefs and celerity in the execution of juftice,
" and their charity, are equalled by few nations.
" *In*

" *In alliances, their word is sacred; there being*
" *hardly any thing they look upon as a fouler crime*
" *than breach of engagements.* *Theft and adultery*
" *they punish with death.* They firmly believe there is a God, the author of all things, whom they call the God of gods; but it does not appear that they have any institution of worship directly regarding this supreme Deity. When pressed on this article, they excuse themselves by a tradition, " *That their first parents so grievously*
" *offended this great God, that he cursed them and*
" *their posterity with hardness of heart; so that*
" *they know little about him, and have less inclina-*
" *tion to serve him.*" As has been already remarked, these Hottentots are the only Negroe nations bordering on the sea, we read of, who are not concerned in making or keeping slaves. Those slaves made use of by the Hollanders at the Cape, are brought from other parts of Guinea. Numbers of these people told the anthor, " That the vices they saw prevail amongst Chris-
" tians; their avarice, their envy and hatred of
" one another; their restless, discontented tem-
" pers; their lasciviousness and injustice, were
" the things that particularly kept the Hotten-
" tots from hearkening to Christianity."

Father Tachard, a French Jesuit, famous for his travels in the East Indies, in his account of these people, says, " The Hottentots have more
" honesty, love, and liberality for one another,
" than are almost any where seen amongst Chris-
" tians.

G 4   C H A P.

CHAP. X.

MAN-STEALING esteemed highly criminal, and punishable by the laws of Guinea: *No* Negroes allowed to be sold for slaves there, but those deemed prisoners of war, or in punishment for crimes. *Some* of the Negroe rulers, corrupted by the Europeans, violently infringe the laws of Guinea. The King of Barsailay noted in that respect.

BY an inquiry into the laws and customs formerly in use, and still in force amongst the Negroes, particularly on the Gold Coast, it will be found, that provision was made for the general peace, and for the safety of individuals; even in W. Bosman's time, long after the Europeans had established the slave-trade, the natives were not publicly enslaved, any otherwise than in punishment for crimes, when prisoners of war, or by a violent exertion of the power of their corrupted Kings. Where any of the natives were stolen, in order to be sold to the Europeans, it was done secretly, or at least, only connived at by those in power: this appears from Barbot and Bosman's account of the matter, both agreeing that man-stealing was not allowed on the Gold Coast. The first, * says, " *Kid-*
" *napping*

---

* Barbot, p. 303.

" napping or stealing of human creatures is punish-
" ed there, and even sometimes with death." And
W. Bosman, whose long residence on the coast,
enabled him to speak with certainty, says, †
" That the laws were severe against murder,
" thievery, and adultery." And adds, " That
" man-stealing was punished on the Gold Coast with
" rigid severity, and sometimes with death itself."
Hence it may be concluded, that the sale of the
greatest part of the Negroes to the Europeans
is supported by violence, in defiance of the laws,
through the knavery of their principal men,‡ who
(as is too often the case with those in European
countries) under pretence of encouraging trade,
and increasing the public revenue, disregard the
dictates of justice, and trample upon those liberties which they are appointed to preserve.

Francis Moor also mentions man-stealing as
being discountenanced by the Negroe governments on the river Gambia, and speaks of the in-
slaving the peaceable inhabitants, as a violence
which only happens under a corrupt administration of justice; he says, * " The kings of that
" country generally advise with their head men,
" scarcely doing any thing of consequence, with-
" out consulting them first, except the King of
" Barsailay, who being subject to hard drinking,
" is very absolute. It is to this King's insati-
" able

---

† Bosman, p. 143.

‡ Note. Barbot, p. 270, says, the trade of slaves is
in a more peculiar manner the business of Kings, rich men,
and prime merchants, exclusive of the inferior sort of
blacks.

* Moor, page 61.

" able thirst for brandy, that his subjects freedom
" and families are in so precarious a situation:"
" * Whenever this King wants goods or brandy,
" he sends a messenger to the English Governor
" at James Fort, to desire he would send a sloop
" there with a cargo: *this news, being not at all*
" *unwelcome*, the Governor sends accordingly.
" Against the arrival of the sloop, the King goes
" and ransacks some of his enemies towns, seiz-
" ing the people, and selling them for such com-
" modities as he is in want of, which commonly
" are brandy, guns, powder, balls, pistols, cut-
" lasses, for his attendants and soldiers; and
" coral and silver for his wives and concubines.
" In case he is not at war with any neighbouring
" King, he then falls upon one of his own towns,
" which are numerous, and uses them in the same
" manner:" " He often goes with some of his
" troops by a town in the day time, and return-
" ing in the night, sets fire to three parts of it,
" and putting guards at the fourth, there seizes
" the people as they run out from the fire; he
" ties their arms behind them, and marches them
" either to Joar or Cohone, where he sells them
" to the Europeans."

A. Brue, the French director, gives much the same account, and says, † That having received
" goods, he wrote to the King, that if he had a
" sufficient number of slaves, he was ready to
" trade with him. This Prince, as well as other
" Negroe Monarchs, has always a sure way of
" supplying his deficiencies, by selling his own
" subjects,

---

* Moor, p. 46.   † Collection, vol. 2. p. 29.

" subjects, for which they seldom want a pre-
" tence. The King had recourse to this me-
" thod, by seizing three hundred of his own
" people, and sent word to the director, that he
" had the slaves ready to deliver for the goods."
It seems, the King wanted double the quantity
of goods which the factor would give him for
these hundred slaves; but the factor refusing
to trust him, as he was already in the Company's debt, and perceiving that this refusal had
put the King much out of temper, he proposed
that he should give him a licence for taking so
many more of his people, as the goods he still
wanted were worth; but this the King refused,
saying, " It might occasion a disturbance amongst
" his subjects."* Except in the above instance,
and

---

* Note, This Negroe King thus refusing to comply with the factor's wicked proposal, shews, he was sensible his own conduct was not justifiable; and it likewise appears, the factor's only concern was to procure the greatest number of slaves, without any regard to the injustice of the method by which they were procured. This Andrew Brue, was, for a long time, principal director of the French African Factory in those parts; in the management of which, he is in the collection said to have had an extraordinary success. The part he ought to have acted as a Christian towards the ignorant Africans seems quite out of the question; the pro-
fit of his employers appears to have been his sole concern. At page 62, speaking of the country on the Senegal river, he says, " It was very populous, the soil rich; and if the
" people were industrious, they might, of their own pro-
" duce, carry on a very advantageous trade with strangers;
" there being but few things in which they could be ex-
" celled; *but* (he adds) *it is to be hoped, the Europeans will*
" *never*

and some others, where the power of the Negroe Kings is unlawfully exerted over their subjects, the slave trade is carried on in Guinea with some regard to the laws of the country, which allow of none to be sold, but prisoners taken in their national wars, or people adjudged to slavery in punishment for crimes; but the largeness of the country, the number of kingdoms or commonwealths, and the great encouragement given by the Europeans, afford frequent pretences and opportunities to the bold designing profligates of one kingdom, to surprize and seize upon not only those of a neighbouring government, but also the weak and helpless of their own;* and the unhappy people, taken on those occasions, are, with impunity, sold to the Europeans. These practices are doubtless disapproved of by the most considerate amongst the Negroes, for Bosman acquaints us, that even their national wars are not agreeable to such. He says, † "If "the person who occasioned the beginning of "the war be taken, they will not easily admit "him to ransom, though his weight in gold "should be offered, for fear he should in future "form some new design against their repose."

C H A P.

"never let them into the secret." A remark unbecoming humanity, much more Christianity!

* This inhuman practice is particularly described by Brue, in Collect. vol. 2. p. 98, where he says, "That some "of the natives are, on all occasions, endeavouring to sur- "prize and carry off their country people. They land (says "he) without noise, and if they find a lone cottage, without "defence, they surround it, and carry off all the people and "effects to their boat, and immediately reimbark." This seems to be mostly practised by some Negroes who dwell on the sea coast. † Bosman, p. 155.

C H A P. XI.

AN account of the shocking inhumanity, used in the carrying on of the slave trade, as described by factors of different nations, viz. by Francis Moor, on the river Gambia; and by John Barbot, A. Brue, and William Bosman, through the coast of Guinea. *Note.* Of the large revenues arising to the Kings of Guinea from the slave trade.

FIRST, Francis Moor, factor for the English African Company, on the river Gambia, * writes, " That there are a number of Negroe
" traders, colled joncoes, or merchants, who
" follow the slave trade as a business; their
" place of residence is so high up in the country,
" as to be six weeks travel from James Fort,
" which is situate at the mouth of that river.
" These merchants bring down elephants teeth,
" and in some years two thousand slaves, most
" of which, they say, are prisoners taken in war.
" They buy them from the different princes
" who take them; many of them are Bum-
" brongs and Petcharies; nations, who each of
" them have different languages, and are brought
" from a vast way inland. Their way of bring-
" ing them is tying them by the neck with leather
" thongs, at about a yard distant from each other,
" thirty or forty in a string, having generally
" a bundle

---

* Moor, page 28.

" a bundle of corn or elephants teeth upon
" each of their heads. In their way from the
" mountains, they travel through very great
" woods, where they cannot for some days get
" water; so they carry in skin bags enough to
" support them for a time. I cannot," adds
Moor, " be certain of the number of merchants
" who follow this trade, but there may, per-
" haps, be about an hundred, who go up into
" the inland country, with the goods which
" they buy from the white men, and with them
" purchase, in various countries, gold, slaves,
" and elephants teeth. Besides the slaves, which
" the merchants bring down, there are many
" bought along the river: these are either
" taken in war, as the former are, or men con-
" demned for crimes; *or else people stolen, which
" is very frequent.*—Since the slave-trade has
" been used, all punishments are changed into
" slavery; there being an advantage on such
" condemnation, *they strain for crimes very hard,
" in order to get the benefit of selling the criminal.*"

John Barbot, the French factor, in his account of the manner by which the slaves are
procured, says, " * The Slaves sold by the Ne-
" groes, are for the most part prisoners of war,
" or taken in the incursions they make in their
" enemies territories; others are stolen away
" by their neighbours, when found abroad on
" the road, or in the woods; or else in the corn
" fields, at the time of the year when their pa-
" rents keep them there all the day to scare

---

* John Barbot, page 47.

" away

" away the devouring small birds." Speaking of the transactions on that part of Guinea called the Slave Coast, where the Europeans have the most factories, and from whence they bring away much the greatest number of slaves, the same author, and also Bosman, † says, " The " inhabitants of Coto do much mischief, in " stealing those slaves they sell to the Euro- " peans, from the upland country.—That the " inhabitants of Popo excel the former; being " endowed with a much larger share of cou- " rage, they rob more successfully, by which " means they increase their riches and trade." The author particularly remarks, " *That they* " *are encouraged in this practice by the Europeans*; " sometimes it happens, according to the suc- " cess of their inland excursions, that they are " able to furnish two hundred slaves or more, " in a few days." And he says, " ‡ The " blacks of Fida, or Whidah, are so expedi- " tious in trading for slaves, that they can de- " liver a thousand every month."—" If there " happens to be no stock of slaves there, the " factor must trust the blacks with his goods, " to the value of one hundred and fifty, or two " hundred pounds; which goods they carry up " into the inland country, to buy slaves at all " markets ‖, for above six hundred miles up
" the

---

† Bosman, page 310.
‡ Barbot, page 326.
‖ When the great income which arises to the Negroe Kings on the Slave Coast, from the slaves brought through their several governments, to be shipped on board the Eu-
ropean

"the country, where they are kept like cattle
"in Europe; the slaves sold there being gene-
"rally prisoners of war, taken from their ene-
"mies like other booty, and perhaps some few
"sold by their own countrymen, in extreme
"want, or upon a famine, as also some as a
"punishment of heinous crimes." So far Barbot's account; that given by William Bosman
is as follows: " * When the slaves which are
"brought from the inland countries come to
"Whidah, they are put in prison together;
"when we treat concerning buying them, they
"are all brought out together in a large plain,
"where, by our surgeons, they are thoroughly
"examined, and that naked, both men and
"women, without the least distinction or mo-
"desty.† Those which are approved as good,
"are

---

ropean vessels, is considered, we have no cause to wonder that they give so great a countenance to that trade: William Bosman says, page 337, *"That each ship which comes to Whidah to trade, reckoning one with another, either by toll, trade, or custom, pays about four hundred pounds, and sometimes fifty ships come hither in a year."* Barbot confirms the same, and adds, page 350, *"That in the neighbouring kingdom of Ardah, the duty to the King is the value of seventy or eighty slaves for each trading ship."* Which is near half as much more as at Whidah; nor can the Europeans, concerned in the trade, with any degree of propriety, blame the African Kings for countenancing it, while they continue to send vessels, on purpose to take in the slaves which are thus stolen, and that they are permitted, under the sanction of national laws, to sell them to the colonies.

* Bosman, page 340.
† Note, from the above account of the indecent and shocking manner in which the unhappy Negroes are treated,

it

" are fet on one fide; in the mean while a
" burning iron, with the arms or name of the
" company, lies in the fire, with which ours
" are marked on the breaſt. When we have
" agreed with the owners of the flaves, they
" are returned to their prifons, where, from
" that time forward, they are kept at our
" charge, and coſt us two pence a day each
" flave, which ſerves to fubfiſt them like cri-
" minals on bread and water; ſo that to fave
" charges, we fend them on board our ſhips
" the

It is reaſonable for perſons unacquainted with theſe people, to conclude them to be void of that natural modeſty, ſo becoming a reaſonable creature; but thoſe who have had intercourſe with the Blacks in theſe northern colonies, know that this would be a wrong concluſion, for they are indeed as ſuſceptible of modeſty and ſhame as other people. It is the unparalleled brutality, to which the Europeans have, by long cuſtom, been inured, which urgeth them, without bluſhing, to act ſo ſhameful a part. Such uſage is certainly grievous to the poor Negroes, particularly the women; but they are flaves, and muſt ſubmit to this, or any other abuſe that is offered them by their cruel taſk-maſters, or expect to be inhumanly tormented into acquieſcence. That the Blacks are unaccuſtomed to ſuch brutality, appears from an inſtance mentioned in Aſtley's Collection, vol. 2. page 201. viz. " At an audience which Caſſeneuve had of the
" King of Congo, where he was uſed with a great deal of
" civility by the Blacks, ſome flaves were delivered to
" him. The King obſerving Caſſeneuve (according to the
" cuſtom of the Europeans) to handle the limbs of the
" flaves, burſt out a laughing, as did the great men about
" him: the factor aſking the interpreter the occaſion of
" their mirth, was told it proceeded from his ſo nicely
" examining the flaves. Neverthelefs, *the King was ſo*
" *aſhamed of it, that he defired him, for decency's ſake, to do*
" *it in a more private manner.*"

H

" the very firſt opportunity; before which,
" their maſters ſtrip them of all they have on
" their backs, ſo that they come on board ſtark
" naked, as well women as men. In which
" condition they are obliged to continue, if
" the maſter of the ſhip is not ſo charitable
" (which he commonly is) as to beſtow ſome-
" thing on them to cover their nakedneſs. Six
" or ſeven hundred are ſometimes put on board
" a veſſel, where they lie as cloſe together as
" it is poſſible for them to be crouded."

CHAP.

C H A P. XII.

EXTRACTS of several Journals of Voyages to the coast of Guinea for slaves, whereby the extreme inhumanity of that traffic is described. *Melancholy* account of a ship blown up on that coast, with a great number of Negroes on board. *Instances* of shocking barbarity perpetrated by masters of vessels towards their slaves. *Inquiry* why these scandalous infringements, both of divine and human laws, are overlooked by the government.

THE misery and bloodshed attendant on the slave-trade, are set forth by the following extracts of two voyages to the coast of Guinea for slaves. The first is in a vessel from Liverpool, taken *verbatim* from the original manuscript of the Surgeon's Journal, *viz.*

" Sestro, December the 29th, 1724. No trade
" to-day, though many traders came on board;
" they informed us, that the people are gone
" to war within land, and will bring prisoners
" enough in two or three days, in hopes of
" which we stay."

The 30th. " No trade yet, but our traders
" came on board to-day, and informed us the
" people had burnt four towns of their ene-
" mies, so that to-morrow we expect slaves off:
" another large ship is come in. Yesterday
" came in a large Londoner."

The 31st. " Fair weather, but no trade yet;

"we see each night towns burning, but we
"hear the Sestro men are many of them killed
"by the inland Negroes, so that we fear this
"war will be unsuccessful."

The 2d of January. "Last night we saw
"a prodigious fire break out about eleven
"o'clock, and this morning see the town of
"Sestro burnt down to the ground; (it con-
"tained some hundreds of houses) so that we
"find their enemies are too hard for them at
"present, and consequently our trade spoiled
"here; therefore, about seven o'clock, we
"weighed anchor, as did likewise the three
"other vessels, to proceed lower down."

The second relation, also taken from the original manuscript Journal of a person of credit, who went surgeon on the same trade, in a vessel from New York, about twenty years past, is as follows; viz. "Being on the coast, the Com-
"mander of the vessel, according to custom,
"sent a person on shore with a present to the
"King, acquainting him with his arrival, and
"letting him know, they wanted a cargo of
"slaves. The King promised to furnish them
"with the slaves; and, in order to do it, set
"out to go to war against his enemies; design-
"ing to surprise some town, and take all the
"people prisoners. Some time after, the King
"sent them word, he had not yet met with the
"desired success; having been twice repulsed,
"in attempting to break up two towns, but
"that he still hoped to procure a number of
"slaves for them; and in this design he per-
"sisted, till he met his enemies in the field,
"where a battle was fought, which lasted three
"days,

" days, during which time the engagement was
" so bloody, that four thoufand five hundred
" men were flain on the fpot." The perfon
who wrote the account, beheld the bodies, as
they lay on the field of battle. " Think," fays
he in his Journal, " what a pitiable fight it was,
" to fee the widows weeping over their loft
" hufbands, orphans deploring the lofs of their
" fathers, &c. &c." In the 6th vol. of Churchill's
Collection of Voyages, page 219, we have the
relation of a voyage performed by Captain
Philips, in a fhip of 450 tons, along the coaft
of Guinea, for elephants teeth, gold, and Negroe flaves, intended for Barbadoes; in which
he fays, that they took " feven hundred flaves
" on board, the men being all put into irons
" two by two, fhackled together to prevent
" their mutinying or fwimming afhore. That
" the Negroes are fo loth to leave their own
" country, that they often leap out of the canoe,
" boat, or fhip, into the fea, and keep under
" water till they are drowned, to avoid being
" taken up, and faved by the boats which purfue
" them."—They had about twelve Negroes who
willingly drowned themfelves; others ftarved
themfelves to death.—Philips was advifed to cut
off the legs and arms of fome to terrify the reft,
(as other Captains had done) but this he refufed
to do. From the time of his taking the Negroes on
board, to his arrival at Barbadoes, no lefs than
three hundred and twenty died of various difeafes.*

---

* The following relation is inferted at the requeft of the
author.
That I may contribute all in my power towards the good

Reader, bring the matter home to thy own heart, and confider whether any fituation can be

of mankind, by infpiring any individuals with a fuitable abhorence of that deteftable practice of trading in our fellow-creatures, and in fome meafure atone for my neglect of duty as a Chriftian, in engaging in that wicked traffic, I offer to their ferious confideration fome few occurrences, of which I was an eye-witnefs; that being ftruck with the wretched and affecting fcene, they may fofter that humane principle, which is the noble and difinterefted characteriftic of man, and improve it to the benefit of their children's children.

About the year 1749, I failed from Liverpool to the coaft of Guinea. Some time after our arrival, I was ordered to go up the country a confiderable diftance, upon having notice from one of the Negroe Kings, that he had a parcel of flaves to difpofe of. I received my inftructions, and went, carrying with me an account of fuch goods as we had on board, to exchange for the flaves we intended to purchafe. Upon being introduced, I prefented him with a fmall cafe of Englifh fpirits, a gun, and fome trifles; which having accepted, and having underftood by an interpreter what goods we had, the next day was appointed for viewing the flaves; we found about two hundred confined in one place. But here how fhall I relate the affecting fight I there beheld! How can I fufficiently defcribe the filent forrow which appeared in the countenance of the afflicted father, and the painful anguifh of the tender mother, expecting to be for ever feparated from their tender offspring; the diftreffed maid, wringing her hands in prefage of her future wretchednefs, and the general cry of the innocent from a dreadful apprehenfion of the perpetual flavery to which they were doomed! Under a fenfe of my offence to God, in the perfon of his creatures, I acknowledge I purchafed eleven, whom I conducted tied two and two to the fhip. Being but a fmall fhip, (ninety ton) we foon purchafed our cargo, confifting of one hundred and feventy flaves, whom thou mayeft, reader, range in thy view, as they were fhackled two and two together, pent up within the narrow confines of the main deck, with the complicated diftrefs of ficknefs, chains,

and

be more completely miferable, than that of
thefe diftreffed captives. When we reflect that
each individual of this number had probably
fome tender attachment, which was broken by
this cruel feparation; fome parent or wife, who
had not an opportunity of mingling tears in a
parting embrace; perhaps fome infants, or aged
parents, whom his labour was to feed, and vigi-
lance protect; themfelves under the moft dreadful apprehenfion of an unknown perpetual flavery; confined within the narrow limits of a
veffel, where often feveral hundreds lie as clofe

and contempt; deprived of every fond and focial tie, and,
in a great meafure, reduced to a ftate of defperation. We
had not been a fortnight at fea, before the fatal confequence of this defpair appeared; they formed a defign of re-
covering their natural right, LIBERTY, by rifing and mur-
dering every man on board; but the goodnefs of the Almighty rendered their fcheme abortive, and his mercy fpared
us to have time to repent. The plot was difcovered; the
ring-leader, tied by the two thumbs over the barricade door,
at fun-rife received a number of lafhes: in this fituation he
remained till fun-fet, expofed to the infults and barbarity
of the brutal crew of failors, with full leave to exercife their
cruelty at pleafure. The confequence of this was, that next
morning the miferable fufferer was found dead, flayed from
the fhoulders to the waift. The next victim was a youth,
who, from too ftrong a fenfe of his mifery, refufed nourifh-
ment, and died difregarded and unnoticed, till the hogs had
fed on part of his flefh. Will not Chriftianity blufh at this
impious facrilege? May the relation of it ferve to call back
the ftruggling remains of humanity in the hearts of thofe,
who, from a love of wealth, partake in any degree of this oppreffive gain; and have fuch an effect on the minds of the fin-
cere, as may be productive of peace, the happy effect of true
repentance for paft tranfgreffions, and a refolution to renounce
all connexion with it for the time to come.

as possible. Under these aggravated distresses, they are often reduced to a state of despair, in which many have been frequently killed, and some deliberately put to death under the greatest torture, when they have attempted to rise, in order to free themselves from present misery, and the slavery designed them. † Many accounts of this nature might be mentioned; indeed from the vast number of vessels employed in the trade, and the repeated relations in the public prints of Negroes rising on board the vessels from Guinea, it is more than probable, that many such instances occur every year. I shall only mention one example of this kind, by which the reader may judge of the rest; it is in Astley's Collection, vol. 2. page 449, related by John Atkins, surgeon on board Admiral Ogle's squadron, of one " Harding, master of a vessel in which several " of the men-slaves and women-slaves attempt- " ed to rise in order to recover their liberty; " some of whom the master, of his own autho- " rity, sentenced to cruel death, making them " first eat the heart and liver of one of those he " had killed. The women he hoisted by the " thumbs, whipped, and slashed with knives be- " fore the other slaves, till she died*." As detestable

---

† See the Appendix.
* A memorable instance of some of the dreadful effects of the slave-trade, happened about five years past, on a ship from this port, then at anchor about three miles from shore, near Acra Fort, on the coast of Guinea. They had purchased between four and five hundred Negroes, and were ready to sail for the West-Indies. It is customary on board those vessels, to keep the men shackled two by two, each by one

teftable and fhocking as this may appear to fuch whofe hearts are not yet hardened by the practice of that cruelty, which the love of wealth by degrees introduceth into the human mind, it will not be ftrange to thofe who have been concerned or employed in the trade.

Now here arifes a neceffary query to thofe how hold the balance of juftice, and who muft be accountable

---

one leg to a fmall iron bar; thefe are every day brought on the deck for the benefit of the air; and left they fhould attempt to recover their freedom, they are made faft to two common chains, which are extended each fide the main deck; the women and children are loofe. This was the fituation of the flaves on board this veffel, when it took fire by means of a perfon who was drawing fpirits by the light of a lamp; the cafk burfting, the fire fpread with fo much violence, that in about ten minutes, the failors. apprehending it impoffible to extinguifh it before it could reach a large quantity of powder they had on board, concluded it neceffary to caft themfelves into the fea, as the only chance of faving their lives; and firft they endeavoured to loofe the chains by which the Negroe men were faftened on the deck; but in the confufion the key being miffing, they had but juft time to loofe one of the chains by wrenching the ftaple; when the vehemence of the fire fo increafed, that they all but one man jumped over board, when immediately the fire having gained the powder, the veffel blew up with all the flaves who remained faftened to the one chain, and fuch others as had not followed the failors examples. There happened to be three Portugueze veffels in fight, who, with others from the fhore, putting out their boats, took up about two hundred and fifty of thofe poor fouls who remained alive; of which number, about fifty died on fhore, being moftly of thofe who were fettered together by iron fhackles, which, as they jumped into the fea, had broken their legs, and thefe fractures being inflamed by fo long a ftruggle in the fea, probably mortified, which occafioned the death of every one that was fo wounded. The two hundred remaining alive, were foon difpofed of, for account of the owners, to other purchafers.

countable to God for the ufe they have made of it, That as the principles on which the Britifh conftitution is founded, are fo favourable to the common rights of mankind, how it has happened that the laws which countenance this iniquitous traffic, have obtained the fanction of the legiflature? and that the executive part of government fhould fo long fhut their ears to continual reports of the barbarities perpetrated againft thefe unhappy people, and leave the trading fubjects at liberty to trample on the moft precious rights of others, even without a rebuke? Why are the mafters of veffels thus fuffered to be the fovereign arbiters of the lives of the miferable Negroes, and allowed with impunity thus to deftroy (may I not properly fay, *to murder*) their fellow-creatures; and that by means fo cruel, as cannot be even related but with fhame and horror?

CHAP.

CHAP. XIII.

USAGE of the Negroes, when they arrive in the West Indies. An hundred thousand Negroes brought from Guinea every year to the English colonies. The number of Negroes who die in the passage and seasoning. These are, properly speaking, murdered by the prosecution of this infamous traffic. Remarks on its dreadful *effects and tendency*.

WHEN the vessels arrive at their destined port in the colonies, the poor Negroes are to be disposed of to the planters; and here they are again exposed naked, without any distinction of sexes, to the brutal examination of their purchasers; and this, it may well be judged, is, to many, another occasion of deep distress. Add to this, that near connexions must now again be separated, to go with their several purchasers; this must be deeply affecting to all, but such whose hearts are seared by the love of gain. Mothers are seen hanging over their daughters, bedewing their naked breasts with tears, and daughters clinging to their parents, not knowing what new stage of distress must follow their separation, or whether they shall ever meet again. And here what sympathy, what commiseration, do they meet with? Why, indeed, if they will not separate as readily as their owners think proper, the whipper is called for,

and

and the lash exercised upon their naked bodies, till obliged to part. Can any human heart, which has not become callous by the practice of such cruelties, be unconcerned, even at the relation of such grievous affliction, to which this oppressed part of our species are subjected.

In a book, printed in Liverpool, called *The Liverpool Memorandum*, which contains, amongst other things, an account of the trade of that port, there is an exact list of the vessels employed in the Guinea trade, and of the number of slaves imported in each vessel; by which it appears that in the year 1753, the number imported to America by one hundred and one vessels belonging to that port, amounted to upwards of thirty thousand; and from the number of vessels employed by the African company in London and Bristol, we may, with some degree of certainty, conclude, there are one hundred thousand Negroes purchased and brought on board our ships yearly from the coast of Africa. This is confirmed in Anderson's History of Trade and Commerce, lately printed; where it is said, " * That England supplies her American colo-
" nies with Negroe slaves, amounting in number
" to about one hundred thousand every year."
When the vessels are full freighted with slaves, they sail for our plantations in America, and may be two or three months in the voyage; during which time, from the filth and stench that is among them, distempers frequently break out,
which

---

* Appendix to Anderson's History, page 68.

which carry off commonly a fifth, a fourth, yea sometimes a third or more of them: so that taking all the slaves together, that are brought on board our ships yearly, one may reasonably suppose that at least ten thousand of them die on the voyage. And in a printed account of the state of the Negroes in our plantations, it is supposed that a fourth part, more or less, die at the different islands, in what is called the seasoning. Hence it may be presumed, that at a moderate computation of the slaves who are purchased by our African merchants in a year, near thirty thousand die upon the voyage, and in the seasoning. Add to this, the prodigious number who are killed in the incursions and intestine wars, by which the Negroes procure the number of slaves wanted to load the vessels. How dreadful then is this slave-trade, whereby so many thousands of our fellow creatures, free by nature, endued with the same rational faculties, and called to be heirs of the same salvation with us, lose their lives, and are, truly and properly speaking, murdered every year! for it is not necessary, in order to convict a man of murder, to make it appear that he had an *intention* to commit murder. Whoever does, by unjust force or violence, deprive another of his liberty, and, while he hath him in his power, continues so to oppress him by cruel treatment, as eventually to occasion his death, is actually guilty of murder. It is enough to make a thoughtful person tremble, to think what a load of guilt lies upon our nation on this account; and that the blood of thousands of poor innocent creatures, murdered every year in the prosecution of this wicked trade, cries

aloud

aloud to Heaven for vengeance, Were we to hear or read of a nation that deftroyed every year, in fome other way, as many human creatures as perifh in this trade, we fhould certainly confider them as a very bloody, barbarous people. If it be alledged, that the legiflature hath encouraged, and ftill do encourage this trade; it is anfwered, that no legiflature on earth can alter the nature of things, fo as to make that to be right which is contrary to the law of God (the fupreme Legiflature and Governor of the world) and oppofeth the promulgation of the Gofpel of *peace on earth, and good-will to man.* Injuftice may be methodized and eftablifhed by law, but ftill it will be injuftice, as much as it was before; though it being fo eftablifhed may render men more infenfible of the guilt, and more bold and fecure in the perpetration of it.

CHAP.

C H A P. XIV.

OBSERVATIONS on the difpofition and capacity of the Negroes: Why thought inferior to that of the Whites. Affecting inftances of the flavery of the Negroes. Reflections thereon.

DOUBTS may arife in the minds of fome, whether the foregoing accounts, relating to the natural capacity and good difpofition of the inhabitants of Guinea, and of the violent manner in which they are faid to be torn from their native land, are to be depended upon; as thofe Negroes who are brought to us, are not heard to complain, and do but feldom manifeft fuch a docility and quicknefs of parts, as is agreeable thereto. But thofe who make thefe objections, are defired to note the many difcouragements the poor Africans labour under, when brought from their native land. Let them confider, that thofe afflicted ftrangers, though in an *enlightened Chriftian country*, have yet but little opportunity or encouragement to exert and improve their natural talents: They are conftantly employed in fervile labour; and the abject condition in which we fee them, naturally raifes an idea of a fuperiority in ourfelves; whence we are apt to look upon them as an ignorant and contemptible part of mankind. Add to this, that they meet with very little encouragement of freely converfing with fuch of the Whites, as might

might impart inſtruction to them. It is a fondneſs for wealth, for authority, or honour, which prompts moſt men in their endeavours to excell; but theſe motives can have little influence upon the minds of the Negroes; few of them having any reaſonable proſpect of any other than a ſtate of ſlavery; ſo that, though their natural capacities were ever ſo good, they have neither inducement or opportunity to exert them to advantage. This naturally tends to depreſs their minds, and ſink their ſpirits into habits of idleneſs and ſloth, which they would, in all likelihood, have been free from, had they ſtood upon an equal footing with the white people. They are ſuffered, with impunity, to cohabit together, without being married; and to part, when ſolemnly engaged to one another as man and wife; notwithſtanding the moral and religious laws of the land, ſtrictly prohibiting ſuch practices. This naturally tends to beget apprehenſions in the moſt thoughtful of thoſe people, that we look upon them as a lower race, not worthy of the ſame care, nor liable to the ſame rewards and puniſhments as ourſelves. Nevertheleſs it may with truth be ſaid, that both amongſt thoſe who have obtained their freedom, and thoſe who remain in ſervitude, ſome have manifeſted a ſtrong ſagacity and an exemplary uprightneſs of heart. If this hath not been generally the caſe with them is it a matter of ſurprize? Have we not reaſon to make the ſame complaint of many white ſervants, when diſcharged from our ſervice, though many of them have had much greater opportunities of knowledge and improvement than the blacks; who, even when free, labour under the
ſame

same difficulties as before: having but little access to, and intercourse with, the most reputable white people, they remain confined within their former limits of conversation. And if they seldom complain of the unjust and cruel usage they have received, in being forced from their native country, &c. it is not to be wondered at; it being a considerable time after their arrival amongst us, before they can speak our language; and, by the time they are able to express themselves, they have great reason to believe, that little or no notice would be taken of their complaints: yet let any person inquire of those who are capable of reflection, before they were brought from their native land, and he will hear such affecting relations, as, if not lost to the common feelings of humanity, will sensibly affect his heart. The case of a poor Negroe, not long since brought from Guinea, is a recent instance of this kind. From his first arrival, he appeared thoughtful and dejected, frequently dropping tears when taking notice of his master's children, the cause of which was not known till he was able to speak English, when the account he gave of himself was, " That he had a wife and
" children in his own country; that some of these
" being sick and thirsty, he went in the night
" time to fetch water at a spring, where he was
" violently seized and carried away by persons
" who lay in wait to catch men, from whence he
" was transported to America. The remem-
" brance of his family, friends, and other con-
" nexions, left behind, which he never expected
" to see any more, were the principal cause of
" his dejection and grief." Many cases, equally
affecting,

affecting, might be here mentioned; but one more instance, which fell under the notice of a person of credit, will suffice. One of these wretched creatures, then about fifty years of age, informed him, "That being violently torn from
"a wife and several children in Guinea, he was
"sold in Jamaica, where never expecting to see
"his native land or family any more, he joined
"himself to a Negroe woman, by whom he had
"two children: after some years, it suiting the
"interest of his owner to remove him, he was
"separated from his second wife and children,
"and brought to South Carolina, where expect-
"ing to spend the remainder of his days, he en-
"gaged with a third wife, by whom he had an-
"other child; but here the same consequence
"of one man being subject to the will and
"pleasure of another man occurring, he was
"separated from this last wife and child,
"and brought into this country, where he re-
"mained a slave." Can any, whose mind is not rendered quite obdurate by the love of wealth, hear these relations, without being deeply touched with sympathy and sorrow? And doubtless the case of many, very many of these afflicted people, upon inquiry, would be found to be attended with circumstances equally tragical and aggravating. And if we inquire of those Negroes, who were brought away from their native country when children, we shall find most of them to have been stolen away, when abroad from their parents on the roads, in the woods, or watching their corn-fields. Now, you that have studied the book of conscience, and you that are learned in the law, what will you say to
such

such deplorable cases? When, and how, have these oppressed people forfeited their liberty? Does not justice loudly call for its being restored to them? Have they not the same right to demand it, as any of us should have, if we had been violently snatched by pirates from our native land? Is it not the duty of every dispenser of justice, who is not forgetful of his own humanity, to remember that these are men, and to declare them free? Where instances of such cruelty frequently occur, and are neither inquired into, nor redressed, by those whose duty it is, *to seek judgment, and relieve the oppressed*, Isaiah i. 17. what can be expected, but that the groans and cries of these sufferers will reach Heaven, and what shall we do *when God riseth up? And when he visiteth*, what will ye answer him? *Did not he that made them, make us; and did not one fashion us in the womb?* Job xxxi. 14.

CHAP. XV.

THE expediency of a general freedom being granted to the Negroes considered. *Reasons why it might be productive of advantage and safety to the Colonies.*

IT is scarce to be doubted, but that the foregoing accounts will beget in the hearts of the considerate readers an earnest desire to see a stop put to this complicated evil; but the objection with many is, What shall be done with those Negroes already imported, and born in our families? Must they be sent to Africa? That would be to expose them, in a strange land, to greater difficulties than many of them labour under at present. To set them suddenly free here, would be perhaps attended with no less difficulty; for, undisciplined as they are in religion and virtue, they might give a loose to their evil habits, which the fear of a master would have restrained. These are objections, which weigh with many well disposed people, and it must be granted, these are difficulties in the way; nor can any general change be made, or reformation effected, without some; but the difficulties are not so great but that they may be surmounted. If the government was so considerate of the iniquity and danger attending on this practice, as to be willing to seek a remedy, doubtless the Almighty would bless this good intention,

intention, and such methods would be thought of, as would not only put an end to the unjust oppression of the Negroes, but might bring them under regulations, that would enable them to become profitable members of society; for the furtherance of which the following proposals are offered for consideration: That all further importation of slaves be absolutely prohibited; and as to those born among us, after serving so long as may appear to be equitable, let them by law be declared free. Let every one, thus set free, be enrolled in the county courts, and be obliged to be a resident, during a certain number of years, within the said county, under the care of the overseers of the poor. Thus being, in some sort, still under the direction of governors, and the notice of those who were formerly acquainted with them, they would be obliged to act the more circumspectly, and make proper use of their liberty, and their children would have an opportunity of obtaining such instructions, as are necessary to the common occasions of life; and thus both parents and children might gradually become useful members of the community. And further, where the nature of the country would permit, as certainly the uncultivated condition of our southern and most western colonies easily would, suppose a small tract of land were assigned to every Negroe family, and they obliged to live upon and improve it, (when not hired out to work for the white people) this would encourage them to exert their abilities, and become industrious subjects. Hence, both planters and tradesmen would be plentifully supplied with chearful and willing-minded labourers,

ers, much vacant land would be cultivated, the produce of the country be justly increased, the taxes for the support of government lessened to the individuals, by the increase of taxables, and the Negroes, instead of being an object of terror†, as they certainly must be to the government where their numbers are great, would become interested in their safety and welfare.

---

† The hard usage the Negroes meet with in the plantations, and the great disproportion between them and the white people, will always be a just cause of terror. In Jamaica, and some parts of South-Carolina, it is supposed that there are fifteen blacks to one white.

CHAP.

C H A P. XVI.

ANSWER to a miftaken opinion, that the warmth of the climate in the Weft Indies, will not permit the white people to labour there. No complaint of difability in the whites, in that refpect, in the fettlement of the iflands. Idlenefs and difeafes prevailed, as the ufe of flaves increafed. The great advantage which might accrue to the Britifh nation, if the flave trade was entirely laid afide, and a fair and friendly commerce eftablifhed through the whole coaft of Africa.

IT is frequently offered as an argument, in vindication of the ufe of Negroe flaves, that the warmth of the climate in the Weft Indies will not permit white people to labour in the culture of the land; but upon an acquaintance with the nature of the climate, and its effects upon fuch labouring white people, as are prudent and moderate in labour, and the ufe of fpirituous liquors, this will be found to be a miftaken opinion. Thofe iflands were, at firft, wholly cultivated by white men; the encouragement they then met with, for a long courfe of years, was fuch as occafioned a great increafe of people. Richard Ligon, in his Hiftory of Barbadoes, where he refided from the year 1647 to 1650, about 24 years after the firft fettlement, writes, " that there were then fifty thoufand fouls on
" that

"that island, besides Negroes; and that though the weather was very hot, yet not so scalding but that servants, both Christians and slaves, laboured ten hours a day." By other accounts we gather, that the white people have since decreased to less than one half the number which was there at that time; and by relations of the first settlements of the other islands, we do not meet with any complaints of unfitness in the white people for labour there, before slaves were introduced. The island of Hispaniola, which is one of the largest of those islands, was at first planted by the Buccaneers, a set of hardy laborious men, who continued so for a long course of years; till following the example of their neighbours, in the purchase and use of Negroe slaves, idleness and excess prevailing, debility and disease naturally succeeded, and have ever since continued. If, under proper regulations, liberty was proclaimed through the colonies, the Negroes, from dangerous, grudging, half-fed slaves, might become able, willing-minded labourers. And if there was not a sufficient number of those to do the necessary work, a competent number of labouring people might be procured from Europe, which affords numbers of poor distressed objects, who, if not overworked, with proper usage, might, in several respects, better answer every good purpose in performing the necessary labour in the islands, than the slaves now do.

A farther considerable advantage might accrue to the British nation in general, if the slave trade was laid aside, by the cultivation of a fair friendly, and humane commerce with the Africans; without which, it is not possible the inland trade

of

of that country should ever be extended to the degree it is capable of; for while the spirit of butchery and making slaves of each other, is promoted by the Europeans amongst the Negroes, no mutual confidence can take place; nor will the Europeans be able to travel with safety into the heart of their country, to form and cement such commercial friendships and alliances, as might be necessary to introduce the arts and sciences amongst them, and engage their attention to instruction in the principles of the Christian religion, which is the only sure foundation of every social virtue. Africa has about ten thousand miles of sea coast, and extends in depth near three thousand miles from east to west, and as much from north to south, stored with vast treasures of materials, necessary for the trade and manufactures of Great-Britain; and from its climate, and the fruitfulness of its soil, capable, under proper management, of producing, in the greatest plenty, most of the commodities which are imported into Europe from those parts of America subject to the English government†; and as, in return, they would take our manufactures, the advantages of this trade would soon become so great, that it is evident this subject merits the regard and attention of the government.

† See note, page 91.

APPENDIX.

APPENDIX.

QUERIES propofed, in the Univerfal Dictionary of Trade and Commerce, by MALACHY POSTLETHWAIT, who was a Member of the African Committee.

I. Whether fo extenfive and populous a country as Africa is, will not admit of a far more extenfive and profitable trade to Great Britain, than it yet ever has done?

II. Whether the people of this country, notwithftanding their colour, are not capable of being civilized, as well as great numbers of the Indians in America and Afia have been? and whether the primitive inhabitants of all countries, fo far as we have been able to trace them, were not once as favage and inhumanized as the Negroes of Africa? and whether the ancient Britons themfelves, of this our own country, were not once upon a level with the Africans?

III. Whether, therefore, there is not a probability that this people might, in time, by proper management in the Europeans, become as wife, as induftrious, as ingenious, and as humane, as the people of any other country has done?

IV. Whether their rational faculties are not, in the general, equal to thofe of any other of the human fpecies; and whether they are not, from experience, as capable of mechanical and manufactoral arts and trades, as even the bulk of the Europeans?

V. Whether

V. Whether it would not be more to the intereſt of all the European nations concerned in the trade to Africa, rather to endeavour to cultivate a friendly, humane, and civilized commerce with thoſe people, into the very center of their extended country, than to content themſelves only with ſkimming a trifling portion of trade upon the ſea coaſt of Africa?

VI. Whether the greateſt hindrance and obſtruction to the Europeans cultivating a humane and Chriſtian-like commerce with thoſe populous countries, has not wholly proceeded from that unjuſt, inhumane, and unchriſtian-like traffic, called *the Slave Trade*, which is carried on by the Europeans?

VII. Whether this trade, and this only, was not the primary cauſe, and ſtill continues to be the chief cauſe, of thoſe eternal and inceſſant broils, quarrels, and animoſities, which ſubſiſt between the Negroe princes and chiefs; and conſequently thoſe eternal wars which ſubſiſt among them, and which they are induced to carry on, in order to make priſoners of one another, for the ſake of the Slave Trade?

VIII. Whether, if trade was carried on with them for a ſeries of years, as it has been with moſt other ſavage countries, and the Europeans gave no encouragement whatever to the Slave Trade, thoſe cruel wars among the blacks would not ceaſe, and a fair and honourable commerce in time take place throughout the whole country?

IX. Whether the example of the Dutch, in the Eaſt Indies, who have civilized innumerable of the natives, and brought them to the European

pean way of cloathing, &c. does not give reasonable hopes that these suggestions are not visionary, but founded on experience, as well as on humane and Christian-like principles?

X. Whether commerce in general has not proved the great means of civilizing all nations, even the most savage and brutal; and why not the Africans?

XI. Whether the territories of those European nations, that are interested in the colonies and plantations in America, are not populous enough, or may not be rendered so, by proper encouragement given to matrimony, and to the breed of foundling infants, to supply their respective colonies with labourers, in the place of Negroe slaves?

XII. Whether the British dominions in general have not an extent of territory sufficient to increase and multiply their inhabitants; and whether it is not their own fault that they do not increase them sufficiently to supply their colonies and plantations with whites instead of blacks?

EXTRACT

EXTRACT of a Letter from Harry Gandy of Briſtol, formerly a Captain in the African Trade, to William Dillwyn of Walthamſtow, dated 26th of 7th Month 1783.

" I wrote thee a few lines the 8th, in reply to thine of the 3d inſtant, intending to anſwer thy poſtſcript, concerning the African Trade, another opportunity. Since then I have carefully peruſed Anthony Benezet's Tracts on that ſubject: whilſt reading them, I felt ſuch reflections ariſe as I never experienced before, doubtleſs owing to my formerly being leſs convinced of the iniquity of ſuch a traffic than I am now. His Treatiſes appear to me incontrovertible, and ſupported by good authority. Whoever reads them, and remains infenſible of the unparalleled injuſtice of ſuch a trade, muſt require ſomething more than proofs and arguments to break the callous membrane of his obdurate heart. Though the love of gain has been the only incentive to it, and example, authoriſed by human laws, has infenſibly led many to engage in it, yet, on ſuch ſtrong ſuggeſtions of its injuſtice and lamentable effects, many, I truſt, who, like myſelf, once approved, would not only inſtantly decline it, but earneſtly contribute their endeavours to aboliſh it, and ſubſtitute in its ſtead, a commercial correſpondence with the Africans, by an exchange of commodities on ſocial and friendly principles; which I conceive may be done to great mutual advantage. Before I had attentively re-peruſed the above-mentioned tracts, I thought (as I hinted in my laſt letter)

letter) I had something to communicate that might throw a little light on this interesting subject; but the many correct descriptions of the coast, and interior parts of Africa, its fertility and produce, as well as of the genius, temper, and disposition of the inhabitants, contained in them, have induced me to think so contemptibly of what I had to offer, that I am now almost ashamed to mention it. I shall therefore reduce what I had in view to the few following remarks and occurrences.

Strongly prepossessed with a roving disposition when very young, I embraced the first opportunity that presented of going to sea from this city, and soon afterwards was persuaded, for the sake of better wages, to go to London, where I shipped myself on board a small snow, belonging to the African Company, John Bruce Commander, bound to the river Gambia; about 200 miles up that river we got our cargo, consisting of 190 slaves, whereof upwards of 100 were remarkably stout men, shackled and handcuffed two and two together. They messed, as usual, twice a day on deck; at which times we always stood to arms, pointed through the barricado, as well to deter as suppress an insurrection, if attempted. Notwithstanding this precaution, it so fell out, soon after our leaving the coast, that some of the men slaves privately loosed their manacles, and rose at noon-day; and although our people immediately discharged their loaded muskets among them, yet they quickly broke open the barricado door, forced the cutlass from the centry, and after a few minutes contest with our people, cleared the quarter-deck of them,

who

who retreated as they could up the shrouds into the tops. During this conflict, I was sitting quite abaft, on one of the stern hen-coops, shifting my cloaths: the sight alarmed me exceedingly, so that I knew not what to do, nor where to go; to advance was certain death, and to retreat seemed impossible. In this dilemma I looked over the stern, if haply I might see a rope fit to suspend me there out of their sight; for either they had not yet seen me, or if they had, did not think me worth their notice: however, by this means I saw the cabin windows were open, and immediately going that way into it, told Captain Bruce, who was then extremely ill in bed, that the Negroes had driven the people all aloft, and taken the vessel. On this surprizing news, the Captain got up, weak as he was, and went with me to a loaded armchest in the steerage, where also lay one of our men very ill: he likewise got up, and with the Captain and myself took, each of us, a loaded piece, first removing the ladder to prevent the Negroes coming down. By this time they had surrounded the companion, and being supplied with billets of wood out of the hold, by the way of the main deck, they threw them down at us, as opportunity permitted. On the other hand, we three in the steerage fired at them, as often as we could, from loaded pieces taken out of the arm-chest. By this means, often repeated, many soon lay dead about the companion; and those who happened to be fettered with them, not being able to get away, of course shared the same fate: this at length so intimidated the rest, that they quitted the quarter-deck,

deck, which we directly mounted, and being joined by the reſt of our company from aloft, the Captain ordered us to fire a volley among the thickeſt of the Negroes, on which the ſurvivors fled and concealed themſelves as they could. As ſoon as this bloody piece of buſineſs was over, a no leſs dreadful ſcene enſued: the Captain having ordered every wounded ſlave to be brought on deck, directed the Doctor to examine the wounds, and wherever he pronounced a cure improbable, the poor wounded creature was ordered to jump into the ſea, which many of them did with all ſeeming chearfulneſs, and were drowned; ſome only deſiring to take leave of thoſe they were to be thus parted from, and then alſo plunging into the water without the leaſt apparent reluctance. This deliberate cloſe of the horrid buſineſs appeared to me, young and thoughtleſs as I was, more ſhocking than the former part of it. Another piece of cruelty committed on board that ſnow, I may alſo mention, though out of the order of time, as it happened ſome time before the inſurrection which I have related. One of the men ſlaves being ſuſpected of exciting others to rebel, was therefore ſeparated from his companion; and being ſhackled and hand-cuffed ſingly, his feet were made faſt to the *ring bolt*, and the *burton tackle* hooked in the bolt of his hand-cuffs: with that purchaſe, he was ſo ſtretched in a perpendicular poſture, as nearly to diſlocate every joint; and in this inhuman manner, expoſed naked to all the ſhip's crew, each of whom was at liberty to ſcourge him as they pleaſed; nor was he taken down till he was almoſt dead, and

then

then was thrown overboard. The consequence of such misconduct, and of the insurrection, was that, of the 190 slaves brought from the coast, only 90 arrived in Barbadoes. This I think was in the year 1740.

My next voyage to the coast of Africa was from the West-Indies, in 1757, on board a brig I then commanded, to the river Gambia, and from thence to Goree, De Loss Islands, Sierraleon, &c. On my return, I was particularly careful to treat the slaves with all possible tenderness, as well from such a propensity in myself, as to give them a favourable opinion of us who were made instrumental to their captivity. And although many of them died by disorders incident to such close confinement, I only lost two of them by other means; which happened thus:—One night, when at sea, an attempt was made by some of the men slaves to get their irons off; being informed of it, I ordered an officer down to examine them, with directions, if he found any loose, to send them on deck. Accordingly two stout men, who had got the fetters off their feet, were sent up with their hand-cuffs on. These I ordered to the other side of the deck, until further search was made below, intending only to secure them so as to prevent such an attempt in future; but in a few minutes afterwards, to my great surprize, they plunged into the sea together, and were drowned, notwithstanding all possible means were used to save them.

My third and last voyage to Africa, was also from the West-Indies, in 1762, in a snow, of which I was master, but nothing more material occurred during it, than that, as usual, I lost many of the poor slaves through sickness.

In these two last voyages, many months being spent on the coast, I had frequent opportunities of going into the country, and once went further up one of the branches of Sierraleon River, than I believe was ever before done by any European. From that excursion, and what I have observed in other parts, I am fully convinced of the peculiar richness of the soil, the great civility of its interior inhabitants, and their exemplary modesty and innocency; instances whereof I saw with pleasure and admiration.

A six and twenty years residence in the West-Indies gave me a full opportunity of knowing the cruelties exercised there on the slaves, having in the way of trade frequented almost all the English islands, and some of the Dutch, French, and Spanish. I can therefore confidently affirm, that the accounts given by Anthony Benezet, and other writers quoted by him, are by no means exaggerated, but rather short of what I have many times seen with horror and deep concern. I do not remember his mentioning any thing of *examination by torture*, which is commonly made by thumb-screws, and lighted matches secured between the fingers, which occasions such exquisite pain, that many I believe have been thereby induced to accuse themselves falsely, and so suffered death in preference to the continuance of such extreme anguish. Previous to execution, in some parts, the condemned criminal is frequently carried on a sledge about the town, and at every public place burnt in the arm with a hot pair of crooked iron tongs, formed to the shape of the arm; and so to the place of execution, where he is either broke on the wheel, or his hands, feet, or head chopped off, according to the nature of the offence. For trivial

trivial crimes, such as being absent from muster, petty theft, short desertion, or the like, the slave committing it is obliged to lie flat, with his belly on the ground, and naked; and if he offers to stir, he is so staked down that he cannot move. While in this extended posture, the executioner, standing at a considerable distance, and having a whip with a long lash, made of hide remarkably twisted and knotted, gives the offender as many strokes as he is supposed to deserve, and sometimes so severely applied, that every one makes an incision. These cruel barbarities are exercised upon them under the sanction of laws which disgrace humanity. The mere recital of them, as committed by a people under the Christian name, is painful. But the evils of this trade, and its consequent slavery, are indeed increased to a degree of enormity that calls aloud for the interposition of Government; and I cannot therefore but sincerely wish, that in whatever hands the important task of reforming them may providentially fall, the God of mercy and justice may grant them success!"

F I N I S.

In the PRESS,

An ESSAY on the Slavery and Commerce of the Human Species, particularly the African, translated from a Latin Dissertation, which was honoured with the First Prize in the University of Cambridge, for the Year 1785. By the Rev. T. Clarkson.

Also by the same Author,
An ESSAY on the Impolicy of the Slave Trade.

TRACTS on SLAVERY Printed for J. PHILLIPS.

AN ESSAY on the Treatment and Conversion of African Slaves in the British Sugar Colonies. By the Rev. J. Ramsay, Vicar of Teston in Kent. 4s. Boards.

An INQUIRY into the Effects of putting a Stop to the African Slave Trade, and of granting Liberty to the Slaves in the British Sugar Colonies. By J. Ramsay. 6d.

A REPLY to the Personal Invectives and Objections contained in Two Answers, published by certain anonymous Persons, to an Essay on the Treatment and Conversion of African Slaves in the British Colonies. By James Ramsay. 2s.

A LETTER to James Tobin, Esq. late Member of his Majesty's Council in the Island of Nevis. By James Ramsay. 6d.

A LETTER from Capt. J. Smith to the Rev. Mr. Hill, on the State of the Negroe Slaves. To which are added an Introduction, and Remarks on Free Negroes. By the Editor. 6d.

A CAUTION to Great Britain and her Colonies, in a short Representation of the calamitous State of the enslaved Negroes in the British Dominions. By Anthony Benezet. 6d.

THOUGHTS on the Slavery of the Negroes. 4d.

A Serious ADDRESS to the Rulers of America, on the Inconsistency of their Conduct respecting Slavery. 3d.

The CASE of our Fellow-Creatures, the Oppressed Africans, respectfully recommended to the serious Consideration of the Legislature of Great Britain, by the People called Quakers. 2d.

A Summary VIEW of the Slave Trade, and of the probable Consequences of its Abolition. 2d.

A LETTER to the Treasurer of the Society instituted for the Purpose of effecting the Abolition of the Slave Trade. From the Rev. Robert Boucher Nickolls, Dean of Middleham. A new Edition enlarged. 4d.

An ACCOUNT of the Slave Trade on the Coast of Africa. By Alexander Falconbridge, late Surgeon in the African Trade. 9d.

WEST INDIAN ECLOGUES, dedicated to the late Lord Bishop of Chester, by a Person who resided several Years in the West-Indies. 2s.

REMARKS on the Slave Trade, and the Slavery of the Negroes, in a Series of Letters. By Africanus. 2s. 6d.

www.ingramcontent.com/pod-product-compliance
Lightning Source LLC
Chambersburg PA
CBHW022129160426
43197CB00009B/1203